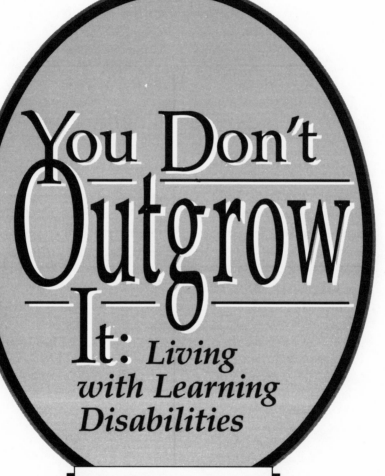

You Don't Outgrow It: *Living with Learning Disabilities*

MARNELL L. HAYES

Academic Therapy Publications
20 Commercial Boulevard
Novato, California 94949-6191

International Standard Book Number: 0-87879-967-2

2 1 0 9 8 7 6 5 4 3
0 9 8 7 6 5 4 3 2 1

Contents

Dedication

to my daughter
Valerie Hayes Harper
of whom I am so very proud
and who inspires me every day

and to my colleague and friend
Dr. Robert S. Sloat
with thanks for his constant help and support

Introduction

This book is written for you, an adult with a learning disability.

You may be a young adult just emerging from secondary education. Perhaps you graduated; perhaps you dropped out; perhaps you were pushed out.

You may be an adult whose parents and teachers tried to protect you from knowing about the problems you now must deal with on your own.

You may be a parent who is beginning to suspect that it was a learning disability that caused you years of pain and problems in much the same way it has been the cause of your learning disabled son or daughter's difficulties.

Whether you are one of those mentioned above, whether you've had years of special education that was more or less suited to your individual needs, or whether you have received no special help at all, this book is intended to provide strategies that will help you live with this invisible handicap that has come to be known as *learning disability*.

I wrote *The Tuned-In, Turned-On Book About Learning Problems* (Academic Therapy Publications, 1974) when my gifted, learning disabled daughter Valerie was 12. She needed some of the advice and suggestions included in that book and served as my "junior editorial consultant" as I wrote it. Valli, as we called her then, wrote a special introduction for the book, and as you continue reading, you will see that she has written one for this book, too. *Tuned-In* is still available after so many years and is helping children and teens understand their own particular strengths and weaknesses.

But Valerie isn't 12 any more. She's now grown, a bright and lovely marrried lady with a family of her own. Just as she has had successes and problems to deal with in her adult life, so do other adults with learning disabilities. She and I have searched but can find few books that endeavor to help adults with learning disabilities help themselves. This book is intended to fill that gap. It is *not* intended as a scholarly work to be read by experts or by students studying to become experts. Students in the field of education will find, however, that it offers a more practical, life-based view of learning disabilities than their textbooks often present. In addition, new teachers or teachers without prior special education training who suddenly are confronted with mainstream special needs students in their classrooms will discover in the pages that follow an inside view to broader understanding.

Most of all, this book is for the person with learning disabilities who wants practical, sound, "nuts and bolts" kinds of help without all the fancy terms and distracting references found in many books about learning disabilities. This is not a criticism of such books – we need them, and we need the experts who read and write them. When I feel that a certain book may be helpful, I have given a reference to it at the end of the chapter. Within the body of the book though, I have tried to include references to other works only where it is absolutely necessary and to do so in an informal way so that the text is not clumsy or hard to read. (After all, many of us have reading problems.)

As you learn more about a learning disability by any of its many names (dyslexia, perceptual handicap, minimal brain dysfunction, and many others), you'll be surprised to find out how many other people share the problem and are finally talking about it. By now the list of famous people from the past said to have been learning disabled is long and includes even mirror-writing Leonardo da Vinci and the brilliant Albert Einstein plus many current government, business, and entertainment personalities. You'll also find within your own immediate world many individuals who have the same kinds of problems you have, often where you least expect to find them. For example, one of my best read friends "reads" all his books in his car – on tape, driving to and from work. There are many others. A secretary in our area who is known for her good organizational skills is very well organized because she *has* to be – otherwise her learning disability would overwhelm her.

We even find learning disabilities in the comics. A Funky Winkerbean comic strip series featured Bodean, the school tough guy, and an active student government officer Bodean calls "Grind" because he appears to be such a good student, always "grinding away" at his books. They've both ended up in summer school – Bodean because he's always failing, and Grind because he was so busy with his other activities, he forgot to take an exam and failed a class. Grudgingly, this unlikely pair – Bodean with his sideburns, sloppy T-shirt, and juvenile delinquent attitude, and Mr. Student Government with his preppie look – have become acquainted. Gradually, as the two warily observe each other, the truth about Bodean's school problems begins to come out.

Grind: "Bodean, do you ever have trouble reading books?"
Bodean: "No – I don't read books!"

Finally, the student leader helps Bodean discover and get help for his dyslexia. The poignant final strip shows Bodean and his new friend going their separate ways at the end of summer school.

Bodean: "There's something I've been wondering about, Grind. How is it that you knew so much about this dyslexia thing I've got? What are you? Studyin' to be a doctor or somethin'?"
And the reply comes: "No, I've got it, too..."

Well, I guess the time has come to admit it in print – so do I.

Marnell L. Hayes

It's More Than an Introduction – Continued

When I was 12 years old, I wrote something I called "It's More Than an Introduction" for my mom's first book, *The Tuned-in, Turned-on Book About Learning Problems*. That was more than 18 years ago. Since then, my mom and I have had a wide range of experiences. All of them were learning experiences, but not all were too pleasant! If you are learning disabled, it doesn't go away – but you learn to cope. Sometimes you cry; sometimes you succeed.

Since it has been such a long time, I thought that an update on my life as a learning disabled teen and then adult might be of interest. After writing the last introduction, I went through some stormy teens before reaching a mellow adulthood, but a lot of learning experiences and revelations have come my way. My mom and I went through some rough time when I was trying to "find myself" and also trying to learn how to cope with my learning disabilities. As a teenager I was too rebellious to cope or to learn about myself. As I grew older, I learned that who I was and who I could become were pretty neat. I now feel that I am a well-adjusted adult who has, through trial and error, learned to adapt my life in order to cope with my learning disabilities.

The work I do strengthens my visual abilities because I am a computer systems manager for a group of physicians. I use my strong abilities to shape my career and try to stay away from my extreme weak points.

I am the mother of an absolutely beautiful almost-teenage daughter, Melanie (who shows no sign of learning disabilities – you can be sure she was very carefully watched by my mom and me for signs of hereditary LD traits). Melanie has inspired me a great deal, too, because she can plunge into any situation and conquer it. All learning disabled adults need to learn that "can-do" attitude!

My husband, who also is not learning disabled, has shown me

how to use his strengths for our family. Also, an event we are looking forward to very much these days is the birth of our son (yes, we are sure it is a boy!) who will be born shortly before this book is published. I hope that I have learned enough over the years to help him if the learning disabilities show up.

Pardon this paragraph if it gets a bit mushy, and, Mom, you are not allowed to edit this one. My mom is an expert in learning disabilities and has helped me and thousands of others to cope, learn, challenge, and overcome their learning disabilities. She knows what she is talking about. I know I would not be as happy today if it had not been for her support, pride, and love. Try everything she suggests. Put into practice any motivational tool she can give you because it does work. I have watched her astound groups of people at her workshops, making grown men cry over what they have discovered about themselves, and teaching parents and teachers how to help their kids succeed.

So, through all of my growing experiences I hope that she learned a little from me because I learned to build my life because of her. And again, you will have to forgive her if she sounds like a mom sometimes, but that's understandable when she calls her thirty-year-old daughter her tiny-bickle-baby! It's because she is a special one. She's my mom.

Read on and learn.

Valerie Hayes Harper

Chapter One

They Said We'd Outgrow It

I hated my freckles! The same adults who told me how cute they were also made jokes about them: "You look like you fell in a freckle patch!" "You know, when they all run together, you'll finally have a nice tan!" "Did you know that each freckle is an angel's kiss?" But the worst joke was when they told me that I'd outgrow them. The joke was on me that time because I didn't.

And we don't outgrow our learning disabilities either. Oh, the people who said we would certainly meant well. Their words were full of hope and wishful thinking and were based on evidence provided by some successful adults. These were the adults who had managed to overcome – not lose, not outgrow, but triumph over – their disabilities by working around them or by working in areas in which they could avoid using skills they did not have. We have learned that Nelson Rockefeller, Cher, Bruce Jenner, and other influential and talented adults with learning disabilities didn't outgrow their learning disability; they just outsmarted or outran it.

So here we are – adults with learning disabilities. Some of us have kept our learning disabilities well hidden in the backs of our secret anxiety closets. We've functioned in school or jobs at levels far below our true ability. Those of us who are female may have had no choice but to accept the labels "dingbat" or "airhead" to cover the confusion, memory lapses, misread directions, misunderstood instructions, or the dozens of other mean tricks our learning disability has played on us through the years. "Absentminded" or "creative" are better or worse labels, depending on the situation. "Absent minded" is a stereotyped but fairly acceptable label for a professor (and as one who holds that title I say, "Thank goodness!"), but it would not be acceptable for a realtor or surgeon; "creative" sounds fine for an artist, but is surely not a compliment when applied to a typist or data-entry worker.

Some of us have studied our learning disability problem for years. Others of us, though, are new to the idea of learning disability – not new to the problems, of course, just new to the *name* for them. Some of us are parents who, in the long search for diagnosis and treatment for our children's problems, have recognized at last our own long hidden secrets. Perhaps we felt slow to catch on – a little stupid sometimes. Or maybe we were quick but clumsy, perhaps too impulsive, mouthing off angrily and often finding we'd spoken too soon and deeply regretted our words. We may have worried about these characteristics for a long time, thinking that they meant something else, or we may have just shrugged our shoulders and thought, "Well, that's just the way I am."

Sometimes a parent will be describing a learning disabled child's many problems to a professional helper, and when responding to questions about this or that behavior, the parent will say, "Oh, but that's not part of the problem – I did the same thing when I was a child!" After several such statements, we parents may begin to realize that maybe the child's problems were some of the same ones we'd had. Why didn't someone recognize *our* learning disabilities earlier? Were we too good at covering up our disabilities by playing the role of the bad kid who didn't care, or the sweet child who got by in life by being so agreeable? Did our parents see us as slow or lazy, but were they never able to see the bright, able children behind the masks?

For some of us, then, learning disability has been a long-time problem, perhaps one we've finally, grudgingly accepted as a lifelong companion. For others, it's a combination of burden and release–the burden of those never-ending LD problems and the release of knowing that we're *not* stupid, *not* airheads, not slow or lazy or dull-witted or any of the other secret fears that we've held for so long or names that we've been called.

If we're not going to outgrow our learning disabilities, we're going to have to deal with them. Whether you've known about your learning disability for years, have just discovered it, or are following a trail of long-held suspicions, you *can* take some actions and develop some strategies which, while they won't provide a cure, will make life a lot easier.

What *is* a learning disability anyway?

Let's start by making sure that we're all talking about the same thing. We'll take a look at what a learning disability is and what it isn't, what other labels it may hide behind, what's known about its causes, and what some of the common (and very familiar to us!) symptoms and consequences are.

First, what is a learning disability? Obviously, it has something to do with problems in learning – that much is clear from the term itself. The problem, however, is that many people interpret the term and our disabilities in all their great variety as meaning an overall lowered ability to learn. They're wrong. Quite simply, they've got learning disability confused with mental retardation. (And truth to tell, in our heart-of-hearts, almost every learning disabled person has had the secret fear that that *might* be the problem.)

Learning disability refers to any one of a whole collection of individual problems in learning that a person with *overall* good ability may have. It is *not* a general inability to learn. As we have seen before, even some very bright people may have learning disabilities.

Of course, it is the carryover from the one or several individual problems a learning disabled person may have that causes such devastation. For example, the learning disabled person whose disability is in reading begins to have problems in almost all other school subjects around third or fourth grade level. It takes a great deal of ingenuity (and, luckily, some of us have it) to work around a total lack of reading ability (which, unfortunately, some of us also have) and to be able to get along in school after that level. Why? Because so much of what we have to learn is given to us only in written form. It can even become difficult for a non-reader to get along in one of his or her non-disabled areas such as math or art or music when written material is part of these school subjects.

For example, when you have to read a long set of instructions before you can work a math problem, but you don't read well, then it may appear to a teacher who knows little about learning disability that you aren't so smart in math either. At another time, when there are no written instructions and you are able to work very difficult problems well, the teacher may think you had been just lazy or careless earlier.

What are some other things learning disability may be called?

There has been so much confusion in the field of learning disabilities from the very beginning, it is hardly a surprise that we are no closer to a definition to which everyone can agree than we were when we started. So many terms have been used to describe the problem that just looking up the early references becomes difficult. In addition, some people may give a completely different definition than others for a particular term. Some of the terms which have been used include:

learning disability (the term we're using)

specific learning disability

special learning disability (I've always thought this was an
    error in typing that became official!)

language/learning disability

perceptual disorder

psychological learning disorder (If you can say it, you
    probably don't have it.)

brain damage (How's that for a scary one?)

minimal brain damage

minimal brain dysfunction

minimum brain dysfunction (I suspect this was another
     typing problem.)

neurological dysfunction

neurological handicap

dyslexia

developmental dyslexia

specific developmental dyslexia

slow learner syndrome

Strauss syndrome

Attention Deficit Disorder (ADD, or ADHD--Attention
     Deficit Hyperactivity Disorder)

There are probably some I haven't included here, but already
this is enough to make your head swim. Keep in mind, too, that
some of these terms have been used for other conditions as well
as for learning disability.

The term *slow learner*, for example, was first used to describe
those whose IQ's were between 70 and 90 – not low enough to be
considered mentally retarded and not quite up to the 90-110 IQ
range usually considered normal. Using this term for often bright
learning disabled people whose learning patterns may be different
and complicated but not slow can be very hurtful. Remember
those secret fears we have all had that we may, in fact, *be* slow?
Using a term like *slow learner* makes us even more fearful that it
may be true. Then, too, some of us have such severe learning
disabilities that we may score lower on tests than our true
potential. A lot depends on the type of test and expertise of the
person doing the testing.

What about ADD?

The term *Attention Deficit Disorder* (with or without hyperactivity; therefore, ADD or ADHD) is one of the latest in the jungle of terminology. Some are using the term as if it were the same as learning disability (which is why I have included it in my list), and some hotly protest that it isn't at all the same that you can have ADD without LD, or LD without ADD, or you can have both. We have finally recognized, too, that you can have attention deficits without being hyperactive although those of us with hyperactivity have always gotten a great deal of notice from our teachers, parents, and others, for obvious reasons. Our activity level constantly called attention to itself.

Dyslexia–What is that?

The terms *dyslexia* and *dyslexic* have been a special problem. In the beginning, *dyslexia* was used to refer to a reading problem so severe and so hard to overcome that it represented almost complete non-reading. It has lately been more and more widely used to mean almost any and all type of learning disability. I have found that when someone says, "I'm dyslexic" or "My son has dyslexia," I must ask just what sort of problem he or she has, just as I must ask a person who says, "I'm learning disabled." In fact, when I'm asked about dyslexia, I very often define it as "a reading problem someone has given up on."

Obviously, *dyslexia* has not been one of my own favorite terms. I am beginning to question my position on the issue, however, and here's why: When the person on the street (or the admissions counselor at the college or the employer in the business) hears the term *learning disabled*, he or she has a notion of what that means, and that notion usually is wrong. Often, such a person thinks that it means low intelligence, and, as we have already said, that is not so. When the term *dyslexia* is used, however, the average person either hasn't got a clue in the world as to the meaning of the term, or else he or she knows it's some very fancy problem that even pretty smart people can have. I'm beginning to think that I'd rather have to deal with complete ignorance than with a damaging wrong idea. It will be interesting to see where this parade of terms leads us next.

Let's discuss what learning disability is *not.*

A different kind of confusion over learning disability has concerned other problem areas that were not included in this category of handicapping conditions. We've already said learning disability isn't mental retardation, but it also isn't emotional disturbance although some of the frustrations and other problems associated with LD can certainly make us feel pretty emotionally upset or depressed at times.

While learning disabled people can also have ordinary vision or hearing problems, neither one of these is the *cause* of the learning disability. Obviously, these conditions don't help and can make living with a learning disability that much more difficult. My slight hearing loss didn't cause my auditory memory problems or my trouble with auditory discrimination, but they all exist together. They manage to complicate my life a lot more than you might think if there were a way just to add up the problems that would come from each one separately.

Lack of an opportunity to learn is also not a cause of learning disability. An older adult who was kept out of school to work or care for younger brothers and sisters may be unable to read because he or she was simply not exposed to enough school at the time reading was taught. That doesn't happen much any more because of school attendance laws, but there are still many adults who have had this problem. Others may have missed a great deal of school because of illness or frequent moves to different cities or school districts, thereby losing a lot of critical instruction along the way. As damaging as these problems can be to a person's educational achievement, these are not the causes of a learning disability.

We should also remember that two conditions may exist at the same time without one having caused the other, as in the case of my auditory problems. There is also the possibility that the non-reading adult may actually have had a learning disability and might not have learned to read even if he or she *had* been in school.

Another "non-cause" of learning disability is poor teaching. Some have referred to learning problems caused by inadequate instruction as *dyspedagogia* or *dysteachia*. Those terms may sound like a joke, but poor teaching is really not at all funny. It is a problem that most of us in education don't like to talk about very much. Luckily, the problems caused by poor teaching usually go away after good teaching is begun if the inadequate teaching has not lasted so long that the student has developed a poor self-concept or missed basic concepts needed for more advanced work.

I keep in my office a photograph of a lovely child I taught in a brief LD summer program more than twenty-five years ago – a child diagnosed as LD who had been in one of the all-white "academies" that sprang up the South about that time. She had been referred by her family doctor after she had spent first grade as one of forty in a rented Sunday School classroom designed for perhaps half that number. Her teacher had some qualifications for high school teaching, but no elementary school training or experience, and no training in teaching beginning reading or math. By the end of our summer program, the child was doing very well. A miracle cure? No. The miracle was that some of the children in the academy class *had* learned to read in spite of the situation. Nicole didn't suffer from a learning disability; she suffered from poor teaching – caused by a teacher's inadequacies.

The cause of learning disability is as hard to pin down as the definition. It's possible that one – or even more – of the latest theories is correct. Perhaps the cause is some minor neurological damage or a chemical imbalance or both.

Can learning disability be inherited?

It appears that there are some types of learning problems that can be inherited, too. There are many cases of parents, children, and grandchildren with the same or similar learning problems. Because my daughter's and my learning problems are so similar, although both her strengths and her weaknesses are more pronounced than mine, you can be sure that we have watched my granddaughter very closely for any signs that she, too, might have auditory learning problems. Imagine my delight and relief when, at age 5, some months after attending the opera with me, she heard a snatch of music on television and said, "Mimi, listen! That's the overture from 'Carmen!'" No inherited auditory memory problems there!

Even allergies may be a possible cause in some learning disabilities. When I had allergy testing done, I observed a quiet, well-behaved little boy being tested at the same time. He was sitting with his mother, coloring neatly and within the lines. After one allergen scratch, he began to whine, to kick the seat next to him, and to scrawl with his crayon unevenly over the lines. After the scratch was counteracted, he returned to his previous controlled behavior. When the substance was reintroduced , his behavior again deteriorated. "You don't have to tell me," said his mother to the nurse. "Milk products. Whenever he gets some by mistake at school, I can count on their calling me to come bring him home. He can't read or write when he's had it, and his behavior is out of control."

Such complex theories as peripheral vision problems, inner ear difficulties, and many other possibilities continue to be explored. Among the many professionals in a variety of fields are researchers who may some day be able to give us answers to these and many other questions about the causes of learning disabilities and perhaps, better still, will find solutions.

My field, however, is education. I have been a teacher of children with handicaps, including those with learning disabilities, and I am now basically a teacher of teachers. I also work with parents of children with learning disabilities. I must leave the studies of cause to others and must deal with the special concerns of this book – namely, what we can do to make living and learning with LD a little easier. In my early days, I felt sure that the researchers would find the cause or causes of LD. Then a foolproof course of treatment would be devised, and learning disability could be cured. Reality hit me fairly soon, however. Perhaps it began to come to me when, as a graduate student, I met the mother of a learning disabled high school student. When she heard that I was a special education major, she mentioned that her son was learning disabled and that she had hired a college student as a tutor for him. I innocently asked if the tutor was a special education student.

"Indeed not," she informed me. "I want someone who'll teach him in spite of his problems, not try to cure him."

And I though *she* was not being very realistic! It was several years later, as the parent of a learning disabled child, that I understood what she meant. Her son had probably spent many hours on exercises designed to cure some perceptual-motor deficit that was thought to be at the root of his reading problems since that was the method in fashion at the time. Probably no work was done directly on his reading difficulty, and he was almost certainly lagging further and further behind.

It's pretty clear that the learning disability itself is permanent, but that some of its results can be circumvented or ameliorated – that is, worked around or made less damaging. We may not know the cause or be able to do anything about it even if we do know, but we can deal with the situation as it exists.

What kinds of learning disability are there?

It is important to look at the many different forms of learning disability. Perhaps one of the reasons that learning disability is so hard to define is that it has so many forms. If there were just one kind of learning disability, and all of us who had it had exactly the same problems, the same behaviors, and the same kinds of interests, it would certainly be easier to plan approaches and programs to help us. That isn't the way it is, however. No two of us seem to have exactly the same pattern of strengths, weaknesses, problems, and characteristics.

What the general public thinks of most when it thinks at all of learning disabilities, of course, is the inability to read in a person with normal intelligence. We have already discussed how severe reading problems tend to cause problems in other school subjects – unless the student is lucky enough to be in a flexible setting in which other ways of mastering material (tape-recorded books or someone who will read aloud) are available.

Some learning disabled people have problems only in math. In this one subject alone there are many possible areas for problems to appear. For some, the problem is strictly in computing–getting the right answer to a problem that is already set up. For others, the relationship between various measuring systems is a mystery. More than a dozen different areas of math disability have been described–and some even have subcategories. For example, difficulty in computation may be caused by perceptual problems (getting the numerals or process signs backwards) or may be the result of a severe inability to understand the relationships between the numbers or some of the words for number concepts–such as halves and quarters and eighths.

For some learning disabled people, the concepts of space, time, or direction may be a particular problem. Reversing opposites in speech or in hearing speech is fairly common. Friends of one learning disabled man have learned to ask him further questions when his answers don't make sense, especially when the question deals with near-far, up-down, or even yes-no. He has special difficulty with questions that begin with phrases such as "Do you mind if . . . " A learning disabled businesswoman has learned to watch herself carefully for yesterday-tomorrow or this morning-this afternoon, for she often reverses them. Almost everyone has said "Good morning" in the afternoon, but with her, it happens almost every day unless she is careful. The problem is not always critical perhaps, but it *is* critical in a situation where she means to say, "I need this done this morning," and she says "this afternoon" instead.

A written language problem, *dysgraphia*, also has many different forms. Many learning disabled people have terrible handwriting (or *penmanship*, as it used to be called). Sometimes the term *dysorthographia* is used for handwriting so poor that it might be considered a learning disability. There is a difference, however, between having problems with the formation of the letters and having problems in getting the *ideas* from the brain onto the paper. This is the problem usually called *dysgraphia*. Some dysgraphic people can produce both manuscript (print) and cursive writing but can manage to express whole ideas only in one or the other. Some can express full ideas in typing, but their handwritten material may be very poor, with incomplete sentences and even incomplete words. Additional problems may be missing words or letters, reversals (backwards letters, even in cursive writing), unlikely spellings, crossed i's and dotted t's, mixed upper and lower case, ragged margins, or uneven lines on lined paper.

One friend of mine who has dysgraphia can write little more than his name by hand, and he does that equally badly with either right or left hand. Only with his lap-top computer is he able to produce written material that is connected and makes sense, and with the aid of this tool, he has produced many superior articles about learning disabilities. Few people would recognize that he is learning disabled until they see his handwritten material. When he sends me mail without using his computer to print the address label, I can be sure it will be delayed because he usually has reversals in the address or zip code.

A person may have both dysgraphia and dysorthographia, but not necessarily both. One highly capable learning disabled woman preferred to write her address in my address book rather than dictate it to me because she often reversed numbers in speaking (as I often do when I am writing from dictation). The address book, however, provided narrow lines in a space only about an inch high and 4 inches wide. It took her a long time to write her address, and when she had finished, it covered about three address blocks and slanted downward across the lines. (She had not, however, reversed any of the numerals!)

For some people with learning disabilities, the real problem may be in learning through a particular sense rather than in learning a particular subject. For example, I learn very well visually (that is, with my eyes) and quite badly auditorially (with my ears). I had not quite identified this problem in myself until long after I saw it in my daughter because the particular school system in which I got my early education, with its visual approach, was ideal for me. I was bewildered in college when French was so difficult when I had been an A student in Spanish in high school. Now I see that the visual approach used in my high school class with much emphasis on reading and writing exercises fit my learning style well. However, the more modern approach at the university with its hours of taped listening lab may have gone in my ears but never quite reached my brain. Later in this book you will find checklists to help you determine the way in which you learn best.

Foreign language learning may present special problems for visual learners because even with a visual approach that uses reading and writing, auditory learning is necessary at some point if correct pronunciation is to be learned. For me, this usually means being able to see the words before I hear them and while I hear them. Foreign language-learning is so difficult for many people with learning disabilities that it is often considered a barrier to college or university study, and foreign language requirements are often modified for learning disabled students.

The ADD or ADHD (Attention Deficit Disorder or Attention Deficit Hyperactivity Disorder) symptoms may present a series of problems that are particularly difficult for LD adults. Some behaviors that may be overlooked in children may not be so easily ignored in an adult, especially when that adult is striving to keep the learning disability a secret. Unfortunately, some of the misunderstanding that results can have serious long-term effects.

The impulsive speaker is often sorry as soon as the inappropriate words are spoken. The ADD adult with poor eye-hand coordination learns to avoid passing a filled cup and saucer with a spoon sitting on the side! The distractible adult learns if background music is a distraction or if it serves to mask outside noise and make concentration easier. Many hyperactive adults get involved in a variety of popular athletic activities to use up some of their extra energy, and some of the medications used for hyperactive children are now used for hyperactive adults, too.

Other problems related to ADD may include such poor or distorted body image that the person is unaware of the position of his or her body parts when not looking at them. This makes it hard for some women with learning disabilities and ADD to know when they are not sitting gracefully, for example, or how they appear from across the room. When short skirts are popular, the problem is especially difficult.

Getting rushed or distracted can cause other appearance problems for people with learning disabilities. A missing button or a food stain on clothing may go unnoticed by a person with learning disabilities as may mismatched shoes, earrings, or other paired articles of clothing.

Feeling shy or insecure in new situations can be limiting to a person with learning disabilities. Worrying about problems in following directions or reading a map, introducing oneself and remembering the names of new people, and handling refreshments without embarrassing spills may make a simple social gathering far more threatening than inviting. I have learned to drink my coffee or tea black so that I don't have to worry about trying to handle a spoon and those little packets of sweetener or creamer, but my terrible problem with names causes me so much worry that I often forget that a party is supposed to be fun. Past experiences of misinterpreting words, tone of voice, or facial expression in new acquaintances may so sensitize the adult with learning disabilities that social isolation may seem the only answer.

Summary

We'll summarize by looking back over what we know or suspect about the various problems associated with learning disabilities. Then, in the chapters that follow, suggestions, advice, and resources will be presented.

First, let's review what we know about a learning disability: It's a permanent condition in which an individual with good overall ability has difficulty in learning and using certain kinds of information, or in learning in particular ways. While the cause may not be known, it is *not* low intelligence, emotional disorders, poor teaching, lack of educational opportunity, or sensory loss such as reduced vision or hearing. Some physical, attentional, or behavioral characteristics such as hyperactivity, distractibility, poor coordination, or impulsiveness, may accompany and complicate the learning disability. There is no cure for a learning disability. A person won't outgrow it, but strategies can be devised to help the person with learning disabilities cope with the problem by using alternative ways of learning, awareness of problem situations, and good planning.

Suggestions for Further Reading:

If you would like to know more about learning disabilities, here are some suggestions:

Hayes, Marnell L. (1974) *The tuned-in, turned on book about learning problems*. Novato, CA: Academic Therapy.
Even though this book was written primarily for children and young adolescents with learning disabilities, I think it gives good basic information about learning disabilities as well as some strategies for determining your own learning style and some suggestions for getting the most out of school. I wrote it in 1974, but it is still just as useful today as it was then.

Scheiber, Barbara, & Talbers, Jeanne. (1987) Learning disabilities: What are they? in *Unlocking potential: College and other choices for learning disabled people*. Bethesda, MD: Adler & Adler.

This book includes a very helpful overview of learning disabilities, including some of the official definitions. You will find that I will recommend parts of this book frequently. It is one I believe you will want to own, not just check out of your library.

Chapter 2

Out of the LD Closet

For better or for worse, a learning disability is something you're stuck with. As an adult, you will have to take responsibility for where you go from here. You can hide behind your learning disability and use it as an excuse for achieving less than you'd like in your life. Or you can see it as an obstacle to be overcome, and you can insist on achievement for yourself, especially in your most affected areas. It is helpful to consider that another course is open to you. You can choose goals that are meaningful to you and work to achieve them in ways which may be challenging, but which offer better opportunities for success by working around your areas of learning disability.

You must decide, too, how far out of the closet you wish to come about your learning disability – that is, how open about being learning disabled you want to be in relation to other people. Will you let it be an open part of your identity even if it means taking a chance that some people may misunderstand and limit your opportunities? Will it be something that you will keep secret, working on your own to solve your problems and hoping they're not too big to handle? Or will you find a way that emphasizes your strengths, yet leaves the situation open for reasonable flexibility?

You may want to make some of these decisions according to the situation at the time and according to your particular learning disability. Obviously, if you are almost completely a non-reader, to hide the fact when applying for a job that would require reading would certainly lead to disaster. You don't have to reveal your disability to everyone you meet socially, however: "Hi, I'm Bob. I'm learning disabled and ADD, so if I seem jumpy and fidgety, I want you to understand." That just wouldn't go over well and is probably unnecessary!

What do you need to know?

If you are going to make reasonable decisions about how much of your disability you want to reveal and when you want to reveal it, you need to know how it affects your performance and your particular learning style. It may be helpful to know what level you've reached in certain academic areas. You know, of course, what level in school you have reached. But if you know that you have managed to graduate from high school in spite of the fact that your highest reading level is only 5th grade, that can be useful. That may mean that you have already learned to compensate in some ways for your poor reading ability by using good listening skills, taped materials, or other strategies.

If you were identified as learning disabled while you were in school, there may be a great deal of information available to you now that was not available to you before you became an adult. Your parents may have copies of some documents and test results, or you may wish to write to your last school for copies of your file. There may be a fee for copying materials, but it should not be excessive.

Remember, though, that not all of this material may be pleasant to examine. You may find some teacher notes that are less than flattering about your ability, attitude, or behavior. If you think about some of the problems you experienced in school, that should not be too surprising. In a time when little girls were almost never paddled in school, I believe I was the only girl I knew who was paddled twice before I got out of elementary school!

There is also the possibility, of course, that there may be little in your records to help you. You may have been one of many learning disabled students never identified. Or you may have gone to a number of different schools, and your records may be incomplete. If you find some material, start a file that will be helpful as you look for new sources.

If "starting a file" sounds too threatening, just get a box and start putting everything you find related to your learning disability in the box. Then it will all be in one place when you need it even if it's not in neat folders. Don't worry if you can't yet make much sense out of what you have learned. As you seek new information and consider seeking an up-to-date assessment of your status, you can always ask for help in interpreting the information that you have located. This collection of material may also be helpful in assisting a professional to decide what sorts of tests to give you to help identify your current strengths and weaknesses.

If you have just learned as an adult that you are learning disabled, some of the problems that you are facing now are different from the ones faced by someone who has known for a long time that he or she had a learning disability. For those who have known about their learning disabilities, the major challenge at adulthood may be in taking adult responsibility for decisions, that is, becoming an adult whose problems are going to be dealt with independently rather than being solved by parents, teachers, or other adults.

For learning disabled young adults who received special services in school, sometimes independent adulthood comes at a later age than non-learning-disabled people. Parents of learning disabled children may have become more protective and may have had to focus so much on helping with the disability that they may not have been able to deal with abilities and the growth toward independence for which all human beings strive. This situation may mean that all family members must go through a process of give-and-take that may not be easy. Both the young adult and the parents will have to become aware that this stage is normal, that mistakes will be made on both sides, and that the result, a healthy, independent adult life, is worth the effort. If relationships become too strained, professional assistance by a counselor may be helpful.

What if your parents knew about the learning disability, but did not share that information with you?

The adult who has discovered his or her learning disability only after a long struggle confronts a situation that may be more difficult in many ways. If the learning disability was known to parents or teachers, but information about that disability was not shared with the learning disabled person as he or she developed, there may be a sense of anger and betrayal that can take time to work through. It will be important to look at the past, but then to focus on working toward the future and using what is helpful to deal with the important years ahead.

If you have learned that you are learning disabled, and your parents never shared that information with you even though they were aware of it, perhaps it will be helpful to talk to your parents. They may explain why they did not tell you what the diagnosis of your problem was. They may have been told that it would be harmful for you to know, and they may have been trying to do what was best for you by following the advice of the experts.

In my early days of work in learning disabilities, I always felt that even a very young child had the right to know what the problem was, and this often got me in trouble with my colleagues. I found, though, that most children, even as young as seven or eight, knew they had a problem and were relieved to find out what it was. You were probably aware, also, that there was a problem, but like so many of us, you may have imagined it was far worse than a learning disability. Do remember, though, that those who kept the facts from you were probably doing what they genuinely thought was best for you.

Learning Disabilities Diagnosed at Adulthood

If your learning disability was not diagnosed until you were an adult, the situation may be quite different. You, as an adult, may be relieved to have a name for the difficulties which you have faced over the years. Just knowing that we are not slow or stupid or crazy has been such a blessing for many of us that we have described it as a feeling that we had a whole new life ahead! Even knowing that a learning disability is permanent and not curable doesn't seem to matter so much when we know what it is and what its limitations are, so that we do not fear that we have more limitations than we actually do.

Adjusting to Learning That You Are Learning Disabled

Learning that what you have is a learning disability is not like learning that you have developed a condition that will produce a handicap in the future. With a learning disability, you are already familiar with the troubles you have been having. The condition itself may be permanent, but it's not going to get worse. Now that you have a name for it, you are ready to find out what to do about it.

For most of us, there will be no need to go through the various psychological stages that professionals have often seen in people who learn they have developed a seriously handicapping condition or illness, or that parents go through when they learn that their child is handicapped. We are unlikely to have to mourn the loss of the "perfect self," the person we would be without the learning disability. We are likely, though, to have to face a fair amount of anger – anger that the disability exists, anger about the time we have lost if the diagnosis was recent. If we can put that anger to good, constructive use in improving the future and in using skills, then it may not be wasted.

Gathering Information

One important step is to find out as much as possible about your learning disability. Remember that file or box I suggested that you begin to keep? Start by taking a look at some of the materials you have about yourself. Is there enough information to make some important decisions about where you go from here?

First, let's look at how far you went in school. If you did not finish high school, it may be important to consider ways in which you might make up for that. It is possible to finish high school in most areas through evening study, either in the public school system or a community college. Usually, if there is no community college close by, there will be an arrangement you can make through the public high school in your area to obtain a high school equivalency certificate or G.E.D. (General Education Diploma).

An important consideration, whether you finished high school or not, is the level of basic skills you had achieved at the time you left school. This is usually shown in the achievement tests you may have taken. Most students are given achievement tests throughout their school years, usually once or twice in elementary school, again in middle or junior high school, and again in high school. Students who were enrolled in special education programs are often exempt from such tests but will usually have been given individual achievement tests as part of the assessments that were given then to help in planning their special education program. This can be some of the most useful information you may find because it will tell you the grade level your skills had reached in several areas.

Again, obtaining information from your school should not be difficult unless you have moved so much in your school career that records have been lost. The best place to start is your last school. If those records are incomplete, ask for help in contacting previous schools. Even if your old schools are in other states, the state department of education in those states can give you addresses or telephone numbers.

What can you learn from your school records?

When you obtain your records, you may want to see how much information you can get from them on your own, or you may want to ask for help in interpreting what is there. You will want to know your level in the basic "tool" subjects – reading, writing, spelling, and math. These will usually be given several ways. You may find grade level scores. Even though a test was given in the 10th grade, for example, your reading score might be 6.1. This would mean that you read at about the level of sixth grade, first month of school. You may find your score broken down further into such elements as word attack skills (how well you are able to figure out an unfamiliar word), reading comprehension (how well you understand a paragraph or two that you have read), or other such skills.

Of course, it is not pleasant to realize that you were reading only as well as a sixth grader when you were in the tenth grade. However, you remember how hard it was, and how you struggled when you had whole chapters to read in history or English. Now you can understand why you had such problems. If you were a poor reader, and someone had read the material to you, you would have understood it very well. It was not your understanding of the subject that was poor; it was simply that the material was not available to you through reading.

Remember that the most important information may be the latest. If your last batch of tests showed that your reading was at the seventh grade level, then the fact that you read only at the second grade level back when you entered middle school may not be very important. The important thing was where your skills were when you finished school. If that was a long time ago, don't assume that's where your skills are now! New testing can show you how much you have gained in skills since that time, and where you might benefit from additional study.

I must mention that many adults with learning disabilities remember taking tests with great annoyance. They remember going into the cafeteria or auditorium and spending hours coping with test forms that were too hard or too long for someone with learning problems to complete. You may remember not taking the whole thing very seriously or just fooling around during the whole ordeal. If that's the case, then the results of your testing will certainly be meaningless! Don't get upset by low scores in this case; just know that you will need an up-to-date assessment for information that will be useful.

Finding Sources for New Testing

If you have not had testing done for some time, and you are thinking about making some changes in your training, in your education, or in your job skills, now might be a good time to have a new assessment done. This is not something you will want to rush into without some planning and some investigation! Testing can be expensive, and the kinds of information you will get may vary greatly.

If cost is a factor, you will want to look into testing programs that are free or low-cost. Most colleges or universities with programs that train teachers and others in the field of learning disabilities also have some sort of clinic or testing program. These programs usually are supervised by the teaching faculty, with some of the testing or tutoring done by advanced students in training. Because the purpose is in part to train these students, there may be no fee or the cost to you will be minimal, and faculty supervision of the testing and report writing usually means that their quality is acceptable and often excellent.

To find our if such a program exists in your areas, contact your local public school special education office or call a college or university near you that offers teacher training programs in learning disabilities. As with any information in this book, if you have trouble finding sources locally, you can contact the Learning Disabilities Association (see page 227). If they can't give you the information immediately, they can make every effort to help you locate someone who can.

If you are able to locate a college or university evaluation center or clinic, you will probably find that you need to fill out an application and send some information from your previous schools and testing results. This is where that box of information that I recommended earlier in this chapter will come in handy. You may spend a little time going through the box to pick out relevant information or what is needed to answer questions in the application form, but having it all in one place will make your task easier. Be sure you make a copy of the form after you have filled it out and send *only copies*, not the originals, of any information from your file or box of information on yourself. Keep the copy of the application in your file box, and later you can add the new tests report to it.

You will probably be on a waiting list for some time before you are scheduled for an appointment for testing. Usually, testing is not done during the first month of a semester because colleges and universities are settling into their routines. During semester breaks, things also slow down or come to a complete stop. Often, the secretarial staff and some full-time personnel are on duty, catching up with paperwork, but activities involving faculty and students generally do not take place at this time. When you are scheduled for testing, the fact that you are an adult may make scheduling easier.

University or college clinic testing sometimes means that the testing will be observed by other students or faculty. If so, you, as an adult, should be informed of this fact. If you feel that this would make you uncomfortable or negatively affect your performance, you may decide this is not the right place for you to be tested. Remember, the reason that this excellent service is free or low-cost is that it is provided for student training. If you prefer testing in a setting that does not include student observation or training, be prepared for the cost of such a private center. It may be quite expensive.

If you do prefer private testing, it may only be available in urban or larger suburban areas, or in smaller towns in the area of a college or university. In Dallas, where I live, there are many such services available here and in the surrounding area, as well as the very fine assessment clinic at the Institute for Mental and Physical Development, a part of my department at Texas Woman's University in Denton.

Another source of assistance is your office of vocational rehabilitation. This is especially helpful if you are considering additional education or training for a job. The high school vocational program in your town or city can usually give you the telephone number for the rehabilitation office near you, or you can check in the government listings in your telephone directory for the number. It may take you several calls to find the person you need to talk to, for offices seem to be arranged differently in different parts of the country. When you make contact with the individual for your district or region who is knowledgeable about learning disabilities, that person can put you in touch with appropriate assessment services. These may be available without cost. You will want to find out what kinds of financial assistance there may be for your education or training, and the assessment may be a part of helping get the information needed for those decisions.

Where to Begin

For suggestions about where to go, you might consider starting with people you know and trust. If you've known about your learning disability for a long time or have received some valuable help, ask the people you have worked with before for suggestions. If a public or private school program worked with you, those professionals will have contacts with university, college, vocational, and private programs that help adults with learning disabilities.

The way to ask a professional for suggestions about where to go for help is to describe the problem, and ask what services would be recommended. The *wrong* way is to name a service, clinic, or professional you have heard about, and ask for an opinion of that service! Most professionals would be uncomfortable saying, "I don't think very much of their work. I've seen some of their reports, and they are not useful. Also, they're the most expensive in town." On the other hand, most *would* be comfortable giving a recommendation of a service or two that they have found to be helpful and reliable.

Do make these inquires *before* you make an appointment or sign up for help. I am always upset when a friend or acquaintance who knows I work in the field of learning disabilities calls me and says, "We're taking Jeffrey to Dr. So-and-so's clinic. What do you think of them?" or "I've started going for therapy at the Such-and-such center. Do you think they're any good?" Professional ethics require that I answer such questions in only the most general, evasive terms. I work with many persons in the field of learning disabilities and, of course, some are better than others, but I cannot continue to work in the field if I am behaving unethically by running down individuals or services. Several times, friends have become unhappy with a program and have asked why I didn't steer them away. I hate having to remind them that they asked my opinion *after* they made the decision or commitment to use the service!

When you are selecting a place to have testing done, be sure to find out what costs will be involved. Again, investigate carefully whether your insurance covers a portion of the costs, if any. Inquire if a full copy of the testing report will be available to you or if the policy of the service is to provide copies only to other service providers. Since you seek this information to assist you in planning for your future, you will probably want to be assured that you will be able to receive this information yourself.

What happens when I go for testing?

Your testing session will probably take at least two hours, and you may even need to go more than once if additional tests are needed.

The night before the day you are to go for testing, be sure to get plenty of rest. In the morning, eat a normal breakfast and leave in plenty of time to arrive at the clinic or testing site well before your appointment. There may be some additional information you will need to provide or, if the clinic is at a university, you may also need to go to a central location for a parking permit.

The person doing the testing will usually spend a few minutes getting to know you and asking some questions about your background. He or she has already read your application but needs this opportunity to fill in any gaps and perhaps to put you at ease. The information you provided in your application has make it possible for the examiner to select tests that will give the kind of information that will be helpful.

Most standardized tests work in similar ways. They usually begin with questions or activities that are quite easy and then progress to a very difficult level. For children and adults with learning disabilities, that difficult level is often discouraging and even a little frightening. Because your background includes failure in one or more areas, you may think that you are failing this portion of the test.

It helps to understand how the tests work. In order to find out how well you do, it is essential that testing become harder and harder until it becomes *too* hard for the person being tested. Look at it this way: If testing stopped while you were still able to get *all* of the answers, you would not have an indication of more difficult tasks that you may be able to handle. Some non-learning disabled students are also bothered by this form of testing, but usually not too much, for they have not had the experiences that you have had which have given you doubts about your ability. Most tests are set up so that each section stops when you are missing some, but not all, of the questions.

Another aspect of testing that makes some people uncomfortable is that the examiner is not allowed to tell you if an answer is correct or incorrect. Don't be bothered by this. It's just one of the rules of testing, and the more closely your examiner follows those rules, the more information your test results will give about how your performance compares with others taking the test according to the same set of rules.

You may be given more than one test. An intelligence test

38

may examine your fund of general information about the world, your understanding of words, how well you observe and deal with certain kinds of problem situations, and your ability to deal with facts and information. Some form of achievement test will measure your academic level in the basic skill subjects of school. Usually, reading, writing, arithmetic, and spelling will be tested, with certain sub-skills in reading and arithmetic tested separately.

If you are having vocational testing done, you may also be given tests of different kinds of skills and preferences that will enable a counselor to help you pick a field of work. The testing helps the counselor recommend the kinds of jobs you would do well in because of your abilities and that you would enjoy because of your likes and preferences.

You will probably not be given information on how you did on the various tests on the day you were tested. The examiner will need time to score all the tests, check the scoring, and prepare the report. If the examiner is a student working under supervision, the supervisor will also need to examine the scores and work with the student in preparing the report and recommendations. Even a professional examiner will need time to score the tests, prepare the report of the findings, prepare his or her recommendations, and have the material typed and proofread. This usually takes a week or two. You may be able to schedule your follow-up conference to learn the results at the time of testing, or you may be asked to wait until the report is prepared before scheduling the follow-up.

The Follow-Up Visit

When you were a child and were given routine group tests in school along with all the other students, there was no opportunity for you to see the results or go over them with someone. If you had individual testing because of your learning disability, your parents were involved in a meeting to look at the results and recommendations, but you probably were not present. Now that you are an adult and *you* will be the person to whom the results are given, what kind of information can you expect?

Most of the information you will likely be given will be fairly straightforward with the exception of the information on the intelligence test. This is still a very touchy subject in testing. Generally, you can expect that you will not be told, "Your IQ score is 107" or some such number. Most probably you will be told, "Your intelligence was at the high average [or low average, or whatever] level." Actually, this is as much as is useful concerning the score itself, but further information on the make-up of that score can be very useful, and will probably be given.

For example, the most commonly used individual tests of intelligence are probably the Wechsler intelligence tests. You probably had the WISC (Wechsler Intelligence Scale for Children) or the WISC-R (Wechsler Intelligence Scale for Children-Revised) if you were tested for learning disabilities services in school. As an adult, you probably will be given the WAIS-R (Wechsler Adult Intelligence Scale-Revised). The scores from this test include a verbal score and a performance score. It may be helpful for you to know if you did much better on one part than the other. In addition, each of those two parts is made up of several subtests. Let's say that you did better on the verbal section of the test and that you did especially well on Vocabulary, Similarities, and Comprehension; your weakest areas were Picture Completion, Picture Arrangement, and Block Design. The examiner may tell you that this indicates that you have good skills for dealing with information that you hear, but poor skills for detail that you must pick up visually. The examiner should include such information in the report, but it is also helpful to be able to ask questions about it in the follow-up visit.

You are more likely to be given actual scores on some of the achievement test measures although this is not always true. For example, you may learn that your reading comprehension on a particular test was 5.2 (fifth grade, second month) when you read silently and answered questions, but 6.1 when you read aloud. This would indicate that you might try reading aloud those things you really need to understand, such as complicated instructions at work or school.

Math scores may also be broken down in such a way that the report will help you understand where your strengths and weaknesses are. For example, if you have good math comprehension, but poor computation skills, this may indicate that you are making blunders or careless errors – you understand the concepts and the procedures, but somehow, the numbers come out wrong at the end.

Asking Questions

As you go over the test results with the examiner or counselor, ask questions about anything you don't understand. If you think that a certain score means that this is an area in which you do especially well or especially poorly, ask if that is so. It is much easier to get your questions answered now than later. If you need to call back a month from now, the examiner will have to re-study your file, and it will not be so clear to him or her as it is right now.

If you have earlier test results from your past schools, you might want to ask for help comparing your last school testing with your current results. Have you gained in any of your academic skills since then, or lost? You probably will have gained or stayed the same in skills if you have only been out of school a short time.

A lower score than in the past may be due to loss of practice in those skill areas. If it has been many years since you were in school, and you have not used those basic academic skills, you may have lost some ground in a few of those areas. Even non-learning disabled women who decide to return to finish college after being away for several years may find they are out of practice in basic math, for example. As a person with learning disabilities, if you have avoided reading or some other basic area, you may have a similar problem.

What do I do with the results?

Since you went into testing with the idea that you needed this information to help you plan your future steps, you can ask how the results relate to what you are considering. If you plan to finish high school through an adult program or through an equivalency, the counselor can let you know what, if any, skills will need brushing up and can help you work out a plan for doing so. If the results indicate that there are some problems so large that brushing up will not be the answer, ask if educational therapy for those areas or a plan to by-pass the problem might be more appropriate.

For example, if your reading is at a very low level, you may want to accept that fact and plan to select career choices that do not require much reading, either in training or performance. If your goal is for a job that would not require a great deal of reading, but the training would entail dealing with printed material, you will want to work out an approach that will allow you to have someone read the training material to you, use taped materials, or some approach other than trying to read the material yourself.

Summary

We have looked at some of the issues you will have to confront as you face your learning disability. You may have to decide whether you will be open about your problems or not. Much may depend upon how severe your learning disability is and how much it may affect your behavior in certain situations or your ability to do certain tasks. We have also looked at some ways you can begin to gather information about your learning disability so that you will be able to make intelligent decisions about your further education or your career possibilities. In the next chapter, we will discuss how you might work on accepting your learning disability, and what kinds of possibilities there are for various kinds of help.

Chapter 3

Understanding Your Own Learning Style

One of the things we've learned about learning disabilities is that not everyone with a learning disability is affected in the same way. In fact, even non-learning disabled people vary in the ways they learn best – not just how smart they are, but the form of the information that they can learn and remember best. Really thorough testing can help determine a person's best approach to learning and can give information indicating if
- visual, auditory, or tactile information is best;
- individual or small group instruction is best;
- what form of assignments can make school learning most effective for a particular student.

Of course, individual assessment for all students in school would be expensive and time-consuming. Schools normally do comprehensive testing only of students who are having serious problems in learning.

I have always felt, however, that at the very least we should help all learners know whether they learn best by seeing or by hearing – in other words, whether they are more inclined to be visual or auditory learners. Just that much of a distinction can be helpful to the individual learner and to his or her teachers. Surely then schools would also become aware of the need for at least two beginning reading approaches in each school – a more visual approach and a more auditory approach – instead of one approach for all learners until some of them fail and must go on to remedial programs.

Helping learners discover whether they are better visual or auditory learners would not be extremely difficult or time-consuming. Even the little things we like and do well give us clues to our best learning modalities. For example, my closest colleague, with whom I do a great deal of joint work, is as auditory as I am visual, and each of us gives himself or herself away repeatedly. I may get something exciting in the mail and dash into his office shouting "Look at this!" and handing it to him to read. If he gets the exciting mail first, he runs into my office shouting, "Listen to this!" and begins to read it to me.

When the excitement dies down, we remember: It's better for him if I read it to him; it's better for me if he hands it to me and lets me read it for myself. Each of us has the impulse, of course, to try to share information in the way we learn best, and in the rush to share, we forget that we learn quite differently. Because I am visual, I say, "Look!" Because he is auditory, he says, "Listen!"

The reason I emphasize auditory and visual learning the most is because after a very short time in school, usually around the third grade, the tactile-kinesthetic way of learning – that is, learning by touching and doing – is emphasized much less. Mature students are expected to take in most of the information they need by seeing or hearing unless they are blind or deaf or have serious acuity problems in one of those two areas.

It can be helpful to know that you have tactile-kinesthetic strengths, of course. There are many things that really can be learned almost no other way than by doing – for example, tying shoes or riding a bicycle. You can also use tactile-kinesthetic strengths to help you get the most from your visual or auditory strength. For example, I will frequently make a list of things I must remember. Often, I do not need to look at my list later, but the tactile-kinesthetic input of writing it down helps strengthen my visual image of it, and I can look at it in my mind's eye. If I am not in a location where it is convenient to make a list, of course, I can visualize making it mentally, but my memory cues are stronger if I have actually taken pen or pencil and written the list.

Our primary purpose here is to help you determine whether you are more auditory or more visual. Mainly, you will use what you know about yourself to discover your stronger area.

Perhaps you already know what type of learning suits you best. You may have had excellent testing and special services throughout school and have a good grasp of the best approaches to use in learning. If so, this section is not for you though you might enjoy going through it to verify what you already know. You might also pick up one or two new hints you can use as well.

If, however, you still aren't sure about your best approach to learning, perhaps going over these checklists will help. You may not previously have been diagnosed as learning disabled, or you may not have had access to the information from your assessments over the years. Or it is possible that you found the information too complex to be helpful to you.

These checklists are intended to give you a rough idea of whether you are more of an auditory learner or a visual learner. They are adapted from the checklists I originally used in my book for learning disabled children and adolescents, *The Tuned-In, Turned-On Book About Learning Problems*. The difference, of course, is that these new checklists relate more to adult activities or to what you know about your school years.

The Checklists

Read each item carefully. Put a check by the ones that sound pretty much like you. You may have to think about some of them a bit or ask someone who knows you well to help out on some of them. Remember, I may not have described exactly your situation, but check the item if it's fairly close.

List A begins on page 48; List V begins on page 50.

List A

_____1. People say your handwriting is terrible – messy or just hard to read.

_____2. You don't do well at figuring out charades where people act out an action or phrase. Mimes, those comic characters who don't speak at all, don't make sense to you.

_____3. You'd rather go to a concert or to a talk or discussion group than to an exhibit of some kind, even if the subject interests you.

_____4. Sometimes you leave our words when you are writing, and you may reverse some letters; you may also reverse some numbers when you write a phone number.

_____5. You can spell better aloud than when you have to write something.

_____6. You remember things you have discussed with someone better than things you have read, and you'd rather have someone tell you or read something to you than look at it yourself.

_____7. You don't copy written information very well. You tend to leave things out or you end up with the material off the lines or slanting down the page.

_____8. You enjoy hearing someone tell a joke, or telling one yourself, more than comic strips or cartoon drawings.

_____9. You don't enjoy board games like chess or checkers, unless there's action or discussion as there is in Monopoly. Games like Pictionary, where you have to figure out a picture, are no fun.

_____10. You understand and remember better when you repeat or read aloud.

_____11. Sometimes you don't notice small details and make mistakes, such as writing things on the wrong line on a form or seeing the sign wrong in math.

_____12. You tend not to notice changes in familiar surroundings or people, such as when the grass is too high and needs mowing, or a friend's new hairstyle.

_____13. You have a lot of trouble following a map. You would rather have someone tell you directions.

_____14. You usually got in trouble for messy work in school. You would rather have given an oral report than a written one, and you'd rather call someone than write a letter.

_____15. You have a tendency to use your finger as a pointer when you read.

_____16. You often find yourself humming, whistling, or tapping while you work.

_____17. Sometimes your eyes get tired when you have to use them a lot, but you either have OK eye tests or already have glasses that are right for you.

_____18. You hate trying to read small or fancy print or decorative lettering.

_____19. Machine-scored tests, where you must "bubble in" small spaces on a separate answer sheet, are a problem, and you sometimes put the answer by the wrong number.

_____20. Sometimes you confuse words or names that look a lot alike, such as *like* and *lake* or *Tom* and *Tim*.

_____Total number checked.

Now look at the next checklist. Consider each item carefully. Remember to check those that sound pretty much like you and to ask a trusted friend or relative to help you with those you are not sure about. Probably nothing will describe you perfectly, but check it if it is close.

List V:

_____1. You often have to get people to repeat what they've just said, either because you weren't listening yet or because you missed just a part of it.

_____2. Sometimes you find yourself tuned out and not paying attention when there's quiet conversation going on.

_____3. Frequently you can't think of a word you need even when you know what you want to say. You may substitute a word like "whatchacallit" or "whatzisname," or you may "talk with your hands" when you are having trouble expressing yourself.

_____4. You may have been in speech therapy when you were in school, or you hated it when you had to stand up and give an oral report of some kind.

_____5. You find it easier to understand people when you can look at them when they speak to you.

_____6. It's easier to look something over to figure out how to do it rather than listen to someone tell you. Also, if someone wants to share something they're reading with you, you'd rather look at it yourself than have it read to you.

_____7. People tell you that you turn the TV or stereo or car radio up much too loud.

_____8. You're always saying, "What?" or "Excuse me, what did you say?"

_____9. You'd rather demonstrate how to do something than tell someone.

_____10. Words or names that sound almost alike, like *cake* and *flake* or *Barry* and *Perry*, are a problem for you.

_____11. You have trouble remembering things, such as what you need to pick up at the store or appointments unless you write them down or make mental pictures of them.

_____12. You like board games like checkers or games like Pictionary or Charades where you have to guess what someone is drawing or acting out. You don't do so well with spoken word games, and you often don't "catch on" to jokes and puns.

_____13. Sometimes you make silly mistakes in speaking or use the wrong word or forget what you're saying in the middle of a sentence.

_____14. You have to visualize or recite most of the alphabet to yourself to remember whether *M* comes before or after *R*, and so forth.

_____15. You'd rather go to an exhibit or a movie or play than to a concert.

_____16. It's better for you if somebody shows you what to do rather than tells you, and you'd rather have someone give or draw you a map than tell you directions.

_____17. You can do many things that you would find difficult to explain with words, such as fixing things or doing craft or hobby activities.

_____18. You are sometimes told that you don't give enough information when asked a question – you usually just say "yes" or "no" and then are asked for more information.

_____19. You often forget what you hear. For example, you may forget to pass on telephone messages or greetings unless they're written down.

_____20. You like to have paper handy when you're talking on the telephone, and you often are "doodling" or drawing little pictures on your notes.

_____Total number checked

Which Type of Learner Are You?

Now look at you totals. If you checked more on List A, you are probably more of an auditory learner. That means you'll do better in both learning and remembering if you use your hearing or re-auditorize – that is, say the words to yourself silently – for as many tasks as possible. If you checked more on List V, you're probably a visual learner. Looking and seeing, including in your "mind's eye," will help you most.

If your totals are the same or very close, you might want to have a formal assessment done and ask specifically for help in working out some learning strategies that will help you. If you already have fairly recent assessment information, it would be a good idea to have someone go over that information with you.

Remember, these are not scientific tests, they're observational checklists that are designed to help give you some clues to your learning patterns. Even if you are very strongly one type of learner, some of the strategies designed for that type of learner will be better for you than others. Knowing that you can help yourself and paying attention to what works for you and what does not can be extremely helpful. The suggestions that follow are designed to get you started.

The next two sections are labeled according to learner types. You should read only the section that pertains to your best learning style.

For Auditory Learners

For auditory learners, hearing and speaking are the keys to learning. Anything that can be made into sound will be easier for you to learn and remember. Even things that start out in a visual form but that can be changed into an auditory form then are more likely to reach your brain.

If you have a choice, always pick the spoken rather than the written information. You'll be able to use taped information to help you learn, so if you spend much time driving, you can benefit from cassette tapes, either purchased or home-made, to help you study.

A small pocket-sized tape recorder can work much better for you than an appointment book or memo pad. First of all, written notes aren't in the best form for your learning or memory, and, as an auditory learner who doesn't notice visual things, you can easily walk right past notes pinned up where you're supposed to see them. Get in the habit of using your little recorder for leaving spoken notes for yourself.

You may adapt the idea for your family as well. You might consider using one of those telephone message machines with the optional family message feature, and get your family in the habit of using it to leave messages for you.

When you're in a situation in which you can't use your recorder or in which you must try to use visual material, put it into the form you can use best by telling yourself about it, either aloud or by re-auditorizing it. Remember, re-auditorizing is saying it to yourself silently. When you practice this for a while, you will find that you will almost be able to hear it as if you had said it aloud.

If you must prepare written material, do it the same way. Plan each sentence or paragraph you need to write by saying it aloud. You already know that you can do that well. Then after you've repeated it several times, write it down, repeating it as many times as necessary to get it on paper. Then read it aloud to check for any parts you may have left out in the transfer from your good auditory memory to your poorer written output.

Even if you have memory problems in both the visual and auditory areas, your auditory memory is probably the better of the two. You can use psychological tricks on yourself to help you remember things, even in your strong area. Although I am a visual rather an auditory learner, this technique helps me: When there's something very important that you must remember, tell yourself to remember it. Say something like "I must remember to stop at the cleaners before I go home" or "Stop at the cleaners before going home!" Be sure you word your orders to yourself *positively*. Too often, we almost make ourselves forget by giving ourselves negative orders. We may say, "I hope I don't forget to stop at the cleaners" or "I bet I'll forget to stop" or even "Don't forget to stop." It's always better to give yourself positive instructions.

For Visual Learners

For you, looking, seeing, and visualizing are the keys to learning. Written words, pictures, and colors all may be helpful to you. While trying to learn from a taped cassette in you car may be a complete waste of time for you, you will find that many kinds of learning are easier for you when you put information into a visual form. Even making mental pictures can help you learn and remember.

It will be important for you to use visual cues whenever you can, especially when you are in a situation that usually means "ears only," such as when you are on the telephone. I have often said that I can't talk on the telephone without pencil and paper. I understand what I am hearing, but I can't remember it later. I have a very hard time writing and listening at the same time, but I know that I must get as much on paper as possible. It happens often at my office that I must take a telephone call and then go on to something else before I can look back at my notes. I am always surprised at how much there is that I did not recall until I saw the notes.

Keep an appointment book with you, either in your pocket or purse. Keep small notepads by your telephone and close to where you work. Even though it may slow you down to make a few quick notes, it is worth it in the long run. One of my secretaries, who has a learning disability, has a wonderful way of handling the time she needs to take notes. If someone seems to resent her writing down a fairly simple message, she just smiles and says, "I know this is important to you, so I want to be sure I get it right." Who could resent such an approach?

You may find that using colored highlight markers in books or notes helps you to learn. Even though I am visual, I find them distracting, but I do like to make a mark in the margins next to important things I will want to come back to later. You will find that many people, even some who work with students with learning disabilities, assume that *all* of us are helped by highlighting. Actually, those of us who are visual are most helped by it, and the most effective use of highlighting is for the person with the learning disability to do it himself or herself! All of those hours that are spent by someone highlighting a textbook for someone else are really hours spent making that strategy *less* helpful, not more helpful.

Flash cards are ideal study aids for visual learners. Often, when you have used flash cards to help you learn, you can close your eyes when you need the information, and you can see it in exactly the form it is written on your flash card. That's why it's important for your flash cards to be completely accurate. For visual learners, being exposed to printed material with errors in it can be harmful – we are likely to remember the errors! If anyone suggests to you a study strategy in which you are supposed to pick out the errors, don't do it! For you, that's like strongly imprinting all the wrong information in your head.

As you begin using your visual strengths, you will begin to notice some of the things that you are doing that help you to learn and remember as well as some of the things that do not work well for you. When you have a problem, try to look carefully to see if there are times you are using your ears instead of your eyes. Then try to work out a more visual way to get the job done. When you find something that works in one situation, perhaps you can use it to help you at other times, too.

Summary

In this chapter we have looked at learning disabilities in terms of your own strengths and weaknesses, focusing on how you can begin to use your strengths to help you. As you become more aware of your strengths, you will find that you will tend to think of yourself more in terms of your *abilities*, not your *disabilities*. When you discover that another way of doing things makes it easier for you, you'll recognize that easier way as a better way, instead of just one more weird thing that makes you stand out. You may even find yourself suggesting new ways of doing things to people who don't have learning disabilities!

Chapter 4

Helping Others Understand About Learning Disabilities

Since 1967, I've been helping others learn about the frustration of learning disabilities through my simulation workshop, "Try a Learning Disability on for Size." I've done it for hundred of groups, including parents, teachers, school administrators, college teachers, civic teachers, civic groups, and national and international conventions of professionals in the field of learning disabilities. I've even done it for the President's Committee on Employment of People with Disabilities and the National Network of Learning Disabled Adults. Once the Texas Governor's Committee on Employment of the Handicapped set up a simulation workshop on a variety of handicapping conditions for the press. A disabled veteran's group ran a wheelchair obstacle course, a group had special goggles to simulate types of visual impairments – and I was there to make sure that the broadcast and print media reporters learned about learning disabilities from the inside as well.

I have helped others use simulations to help normal learners experience the difficulties you and I go through daily. I've seen imitations of my original workshop all over the country, and while I might be somewhat annoyed that I'm not given credit, I can be glad that perhaps some parent is learning why his son can't stay on the line when he writes his name or some teacher understands why a student just can't keep from moving her lips when she reads.

You may be able to use some simple simulations to help those who are important in your life understand what it's like to be learning disabled. While you may not be able to simulate the exact learning disability you have, if you can help a person who learns normally go through a variety of simple tasks with a simulated learning disability, he or she can more easily understand how it is that you are so capable in some areas and must struggle so much in other areas.

A simple task I like to begin with is a mirror tracing task. With a fine-point felt-tip pen, draw a few swirling lines on a piece of paper, or copy the figure below.

Figure 1

Set up a mirror at the top of the paper – either a small mirror on a stand or prop up a mirror with a few books. Hold up a piece of cardboard at the bottom of the page so that the design cannot be seen directly, but only in the mirror. I usually cover the design with a piece of tracing paper, but if you don't have one, just have your "victim" attempt to trace the design with a pencil so that his markings will be easy to tell from the original design. You will want to hold the cardboard shield carefully so that the person doing the tracing cannot see the paper except in the mirror.

60

Figure 2

After your victim struggles for a while, ask for his or her name to be written at the top of the page. You'll find that many people cannot locate the top and can't even produce all the letters in their own names correctly! The struggle most people experience with this task is rather like that of a person with dysgraphia, a severe written language problem, or those of us with eye-hand coordination problems.

Another good simulation is to use a story with all the vowels left out. You might use something like the story found on page 66 at the end of this chapter.

Tell your friend or family member to read the story aloud. As the reader tries to work out the words, you should have the full story with the vowels included in front of you so that you can supply the words he or she can't figure out. Keep urging the reader to hurry up and to read with expression. After the story is finished or when the reader gives up, talk about the feeling of having difficulty with a simple task that others find easy. This is a children's story, yet adults will have trouble with the vowels left out even though they may have been reading fluently for years and years.

The story in plain English, for you to use to cue your friend or family member, appears on page 67 at the end of this chapter.

Another good way to stimulate a reading problem is to use some written material that is printed backwards. You can use the story "Three Billy Goats Gruff," which I have included on page 68 at the end of this chapter. It is already printed backwards. Or you can use other material of your own choosing. It may be more fun to use your own material because you can select something very familiar to your audience, but make it hard for them. You might choose a written joke from a magazine, a typed letter from a family member or possibly a memo from work.

Here's how to do it. Take the material you have selected and make a clear copy of it on a photocopy machine. Now you will need to make a transparency. If you don't have access to a photocopy machine that makes transparencies, go to a copy center. Have the copy center make a transparency for you from the material you selected. (The cost is probably under a dollar.) Then make a copy of the *wrong* side of the transparency, and you will have the material written backwards like the story on page 68 at the end of this chapter.

Ask your audience to try to read the material from right to left. Don't let anyone hold the paper up to the light or use a mirror! Most people, even very good readers, find reading this backwards material very difficult and slow. After struggling with it themselves, they are more understanding of those of us who read poorly and slowly.

If you can't read my version of the "Three Billy Goats Gruff," just hold the page up to a mirror. You'll find it much easier!

One way to simulate some of the confusions that many of us have with directions is to play "Simon Says" with left-right, up-down, and backwards-forwards reversed. It works like this: Ask the person or people who are experiencing the simulation to stand facing you. Tell them that they are to follow your directions when you say "Simon says," but that all of the directions are reversed.

For example, if you say, "Simon says, 'Take three steps backwards,'" the person should take three steps *forward*. If you say, "Simon says 'Raise you right hand,'" the person should raise his or her *left* hand. Of course, if you say "Take three steps backwards" or "Raise your right hand" without first saying "Simon says," they should do nothing. They will have to remember to listen for "Simon says" *and* remember to reverse all the directions at the same time. I think they will be a little more understanding in the future!

You can also give arithmetic directions but change the meanings of the directions. Tell them that when you say "plus," they are to subtract; when you say "minus" they are to add; "times" means "divided by" and "divided by" means "times." You may want to use pencil and paper or you may want your audience to work the problems in their heads. Don't give them very much time. Here's an example:

"3 plus 1, minus three, divided by 2, times 5." (Reversed: $3 - 1 + 3 \times 2 \div 5$)

The answer should be 2. You can make up more problems but write them down and work them out carefully ahead of time or you won't be able to tell if your students are getting them right!

I use a number of other simulations in my workshop, of source, but some of them are a little difficult to do if you don't have special equipment. However, with these few tricks I have shared with you, you can help someone close to you understand how difficult some things are for you. Just feeling those frustrations for a little while often makes a person begin to look at things from your point of view and may make him or her more willing to continue to try to learn more about the frustrations of a learning disability.

Suggested Readings to Help Others Understand

1. Barbara Cordoni's *Living with a Learning Disability*,
   published in 1987 and revised in 1990, focuses especially on
   social living problems faced by learning disabled children,
   adolescents, and adults. Many stories of real people are
   included, and there is a resource section. The book is
   available from Southern Illinois University Press or through
   the Learning Disabilities Association of America.

2. Sally L. Smith's *Succeeding Against the Odds: Strategies and
   Insights from the Learning Disabled* was published by Jeremy
   P. Tarcher, Inc., in 1991. This book, by the author of the very
   popular *No Easy Answers: The Learning Disabled Child at
   Home and at School*, is wonderfully full of the experiences of
   learning disabled people. Many suggestions in both social and
   practical areas are included.

3. Eileen Simpson's 1979 book, *Reversals: A Personal Account
   of Victory Over Dyslexia*, published by Houghton Mifflin, is a
   full-scale work on the experiences of this remarkable woman.
   Her recounting of the day that she discovered she could not
   read is riveting. She learned she could not read on the first day
   in a new school when she was called on to stand up and read.
   She had been in a parochial school where the children read as
   a group, and until the transfer, she was unaware that she had
   been merely repeating what the others said, half a beat behind.
   Her struggles and eventual triumph are well worth reading.

Summary

Helping those close to you understand that your way of
learning and doing things is not just different but necessary may
be an emotional experience for everyone. Someone who cares

about you may think he or she understands what you've gone through all these years, but when he or she actually experiences the struggle of a learning disability, there may be a new depth of understanding. With family or close friends, a few tears and a hug or two may result as well. With co-workers, your teachers, or your fellow students, the new understanding can result in more tolerance not just for you, but also for others who learn and work differently.

Th Stry f th Thr Lttl Pgs

nc pn tm thr wr thr lttl pgs wh lvd wth thr mthr n lttl hs n th wds. n d thr mthr sd t thm, "ts tm y wnt t nt th wrld n yr wn."

s th thr lttl pgs wnt t t bld thr hss. Th frst lttl pg fnd sm strw, s h blt hs hs f strw. Th scnd lttl pg fnd sm stcks, s h blt hs hs f stcks. Th thrd lttl pg fnd sm brks, s h blt hs hs f brks.

n dy th wlf cm lng. H knckd n th frst lttl pg's dr nd sd, "Lttl pg, lttl pg, lt m cm n." nd th lttl pg sd, "n, n, nt b th hr f m chnn-chn-chn." S th wlf hffd, nd h pffd, nd h blw th hs n, nd h t th lttl pg ll p.

H knckd n th dr nd sd, "Lttl pg, lttl pg,,lt m cm n." nd th lttl pg sd, "n, n, nt b th hr f m chnn-chn-chn." S th wlf hffd, nd h pffd, nd h blw th hs n, nd h t th lttl ph ll p.

Thn th wlf cm t th hs f th thrd lttl pg. H knckd n th thrd dr nd sd, "Lttl pg, lttl pg, lt m cm n." nd th lttl pg sd, "n, n, nt b th hr f m chnn-chn-chn." S th wlf hffd, nd h pffd, nd h pffd, nd h hffd, bt h cldnt blw th thrd lttl pg's hs dw.

Th wlf clmbd p n th rf f th hs, nd bgn t clmb dn th chmny. Th lttl pg hrd hm, nd pt bg pt f wtr n th fr. Whn th wlf cm dn th chmny, h fll nt th pt. Th pg pt ld n th pt, nd sn hd wlf stw fr dnnr!

Th nd

66

The Story of the Three Little Pigs

Once upon a time there were three little pigs who lived with their mother in a little house in the woods. One day their mother said to them, It's time you went out into the world on your own."

So the three little pigs went out to build their houses. The first little pig found some straw, so he built his house of straw. The second little pig found some sticks, so he built his house of sticks. the third little pig found some bricks, so he built his house of bricks.

One day the wolf came along. He knocked on the first little pig's door and said, "Little pig, little pig, let me come in." And the little pig said, "No, no, not by the hair of my chinny-chin-chin." So the wolf huffed, and he puffed, and he blew the house in, and he ate the little pig all up.

The the wolf came to the house of the second little pig. He knocked on the door and said, "Little pig, little pig, let me come in." And the little pig said, "No, no, not by the hair of my chinny-chin-chin." So the wolf huffed, and he puffed, and he blew the house in, and he ate the little pig all up.

Then the wolf came to the house of the third little pig. He knocked on the door and said, "Little pig, little pig, let me come in." And the little pig said, "No, no, not by the hair of my chinny-chin-chin." So the wolf huffed, and he puffed, and he puffed, and he huffed, but he couldn't blow the third little pig's house down.

The wolf climbed up on the roof of the house, and began to climb down the chimney. The little pig heard him, and put a big pot of water on the fire. When the wolf came down the chimney, he fell into the pot. The pig put the lid on the pot, and soon had wolf stew for dinner.

The End

Three Billy Goats Gruff

Once there were three billy goats who lived across a
ravine from a lovely green meadow of delicious green grass.
The billy goats wanted to eat the grass. But under the
bridge across the ravine lived a ferocious troll!
One day the littlest billy goat, Little Tiny Billy Goat
Gruff, said, "I'm going across. I'm not afraid!"
So he began to walk trippety-trippety-trippety across
the bridge. Suddenly a loud voice said, "Who's that going
across my bridge?"

"It is only I, Little Tiny Billy Goat Gruff!"

"Well," said the troll, "I'm going to come up there and
gobble you up!"

"Oh, no," said the billy goat. "I'm little and tiny.
Why don't you wait for my brother, Middle-sized Billy Goat
Gruff. He's ever so much bigger and tenderer and juicier
than I am!"

"Oh, all right," said the troll. "You may pass."
So the littlest billy goat crossed to the meadow, and
began to eat the tender green grass . . . . .

And so goes the story. At the end, of course, Great
Big Billy Goat Gruff fights the troll and knocks him into
the river at the bottom of the ravine, and the Three Billy
Goats Gruff may not cross into the meadow as often as they
like!

68

Chapter 5

Surviving and Accepting

Certainly, finding out that you have a learning disability is no fun. It *can* be a great relief, however, especially if you have been secretly afraid that what was wrong with you was that you were stupid or crazy. Discovering that what is really wrong isn't either of those fearful possibilities can work wonders for the way you view yourself. But accepting your learning disability doesn't mean accepting a view of yourself as a second-class citizen. It just gives you a realistic base from which to plan strategies to reach your goals.

I used to be involved in testing children who were having trouble in school. In those days, it was rare that anyone ever asked the child what he or she thought was wrong or gave the child any of the results of testing. It was no wonder that many children feared going for testing! Many testing centers looked like doctors' offices, and I often had to reassure children that I was not a "shot doctor"!

I always made it a point to talk to the children I tested before the testing and after it as well. Very often a child thought he was being tested because he was bad and would be punished. One thing I found, though, was that every child I tested knew that *something* was wrong. The problem was that most had a mistaken idea about what it was that was wrong. Most thought that they were slow or retarded, and they were doing everything they could to keep this secret from their parents.

Some students with learning disabilities developed terrible behavior problems, preferring to have their teachers and parents think they simply *wouldn't* do school tasks rather than let out the secret that they *couldn't* do those tasks. They often ended up thinking that they were emotionally disturbed or "crazy," as they often put it, as well as slow or retarded. Their behavior sometimes made their teachers and parents wonder about their real abilities and feelings, too.

The Right to Know

When I let children know that the results of the tests I had given them showed that they were not retarded and not emotionally disturbed, the relief they expressed made me sure that my decision to share this information was a wise one. As I mentioned in an earlier chapter, many of my colleagues disagree with me about this. I have never regretted sharing this information with a child, however. I found that once a learning disabled child knew what the real problem was and that there were ways of working with his or her strengths and around the weaknesses, great changes in the level of effort, achievement, and self-concept often took place.

Some parents of children with learning disabilities fear that somehow they are responsible for their children's feelings of insecurity. I recently tested a very bright six-year-old boy who felt that he was not capable. He was convinced that both his parents felt he was smart, and he was terribly afraid that he would let them down when they "found out" he was not smart. As is my usual procedure, I let him know that he was doing very well indeed, that the tests would help find ways to help him learn better, but that, in fact, he had just finished a part of the test that showed me he knew some words at a teen-aged level! I did miss the boat on one score with this youngster, however. I told him that we would try to use the information from the tests to help make school (which he said he hated) as easy for him as fishing (which he had told me he liked). Apparently he was feeling extremely confident on this subject, for he began an animated discussion about the difficulties involved in fishing: "You think fishing is *easy*? Well, it's not! You have to know what you're doing . . . " Perhaps I was the one who learned a thing or two that day.

70

What if you've known about your problem for a long time?

As we said at the beginning of this book, you may have known for years about your learning disability. If so, then you have probably already come to some level of acceptance of it. If not, maybe the rest of this chapter will be helpful to you. If you feel you are past the survival stage and well into accept-ance, why don't you skim over the information here to see if there's anything you might want to read more closely and then go on to the next chapter?

What if you've just discovered your learning disability?

Maybe you are someone who has just found out about your learning disability. Maybe it isn't easy for you to accept. It can be difficult to deal with finding out that you have something so serious that it's considered a disability even if you have been struggling with the problems it has caused you for a long time. Nobody likes to get such bad news. It would be a lot easier to learn that this problem could be overcome if you could just take this pill or try that strategy or work just a certain amount harder for a set period of time. A learning disability isn't like that, though, and like it or not, it's something we have to learn to live with. Accepting the problem isn't something that happens overnight. More often we adjust step-by-step, in stages.

Stages of Adjusting to a Learning Disability

There are stages people go through when they get bad news, such as news about their own or their child's illness or disability. Many studies have been done on these stages, but I know of no research on the stages one might go through as an adult who has had learning problems for a long time but who has only recently been given a name for these problems. I believe the stages in such cases are different.

Denial

First, when a parent is told that the new baby has a serious handicap or a person is told that he or she has a devastating illness, the response is often to think that it can't possibly be true: "This can't be happening!" This is called *denial*. I don't think most learning disabled adults have that response. We've known for years that we had problems; we knew the things we could not do; we just didn't know *why*. Often, the first reaction of a learning disabled adult on receiving the confirmed diagnosis is, "So *that's* it!" It's a good feeling to know that you are ready to move beyond "Why can't I do this? Everybody else can!" to "OK, so what do I do now?" It's as if the diagnosis gives us permission to move on with our lives. We can't change the fact of the learning disability; what we can change is what we're going to do next. We don't have to keep wondering or fearing the worst, whatever we may consider the worst to be.

Diagnosis-Shopping

When parents have a child with problems, they often continue to look for other different, less painful answers to the problem. It's as if they feel that they can get a better, more bearable diagnosis if they keep looking. Your parents may have done this when you had trouble in school. They may have taken you to many different experts, looking for different answers. Perhaps they hoped that sooner or later some expert would say you really didn't have a problem, or that what was wrong would go away. Perhaps they thought your problems were, or might develop into, something worse than they were, and maybe they were relieved to find out at last what the problem actually was.

72

When it's for ourselves rather than our children that we are seeking answers, it may be easier. Once we have the big answer, a learning disability, and the little answers, exactly what types and to what degree (discussed in Chapter 2), we are usually ready to move on.

But what if you're not ready? I've said that I think most learning disabled adults are relieved to find out what the problem actually is, but what if you're one of the few who just can't believe it? Perhaps you want to question the diagnosis. Maybe you want to keep looking for someone who'll say you're really OK, that you're not learning disabled. Although few of us do that after so many years of problems in childhood and the teen years, you may have accepted only that *something* was wrong but are unwilling to accept that it may be something permanent. If thinking about a learning disability still makes you angry, if you still get upset and feel that "it isn't fair," or if living with your learning disability (or whatever you may want to call this problem) just seems too much at times, then it wouldn't hurt to think about seeing a counselor. And, no, it doesn't mean you are emotionally disturbed. Many normal people get occasional help in dealing with the pressures of life. I have found it wonderfully helpful in my own life. We'll talk about counseling at the end of this chapter because it can be helpful for many of us, including those who are not learning disabled!

Negotiation

One of the stages some people go through in dealing with a major problem is *negotiation*. For people who are facing the diagnosis of a dread disease, negotiation may take other forms, such as praying, "OK, God, if you'll just make this go away, I promise I'll be a good person forever!" For learning disabled people, negotiation may take the form of something like the following: "OK, so it looks as if I probably will never be good in math. Maybe becoming an accountant in my dad's firm is out. But

I have good skills with people, so perhaps office management is more for me. I could still end up in the firm, if that's important to me." Or "I know that with my reading problem, bad grades, and poor test-taking ability, I can't get into law school. Maybe I can be a para-legal." Sometimes the negotiation we do is realistic. Sometimes it's not. But the dreams of people who are not learning disabled can often be unrealistic, too. I know one very bright middle schooler whose parents were frustrated when she gave school very little effort and kept passing up academic electives because she planned to become a rock star. When it was pointed out that she had no musical skills or dancing ability, she quickly negotiated: "Well, then I'll be a Hollywood star – an actress!" No amount of explanation of the skills – and luck – necessary for such a career and no amount of pointing out the odds against this move would sway her.

Acceptance

The stage of *acceptance* is an important one. Acceptance doesn't mean giving up or limiting oneself to low expectations. It's really only when we have accepted the facts of our disabilities that we are able to begin working on doing something about them. After all, taking steps to work on our strengths and limit the effect of our weaknesses is what's going to make it possible for us to function in the world. Unfortunately, some people never reach this stage. Some people are so angry at the unfairness of life with a disability that they cannot accept it, and they continue to fight inappropriate battles, losing precious time that they might have spent in fulfilling worthwhile endeavors.

Accepting your learning disability means letting go of anger and unrealistic expectations that the disability will go away. It means knowing that you are not a less valuable or worthwhile person because of your disability. It also means knowing that you are not necessarily a hero when you accomplish your goals. Working out a brilliant system to enable you to get an important project done at work without interference from your learning disability may be a triumph for you, but don't expect your boss to see it as a finer performance than it would have been had the project been done by your non-learning disabled fellow worker.

In some cases, our parents may have unwittingly trained us to expect others to recognize the times we overcome our disabilities as opportunities for something other than personal satisfaction. When we were able to pass a spelling test or get through a grading period without failing a subject, it may have been cause for such celebration and reward that we may have forgotten that in the real world, results rather than effort are what is sought and valued.

Some of our parents' excesses of praise over our triumphs may have caused problems for our brothers and sisters, too. People with learning disabilities know how hard it was to watch a non-learning disabled sibling succeed with little effort but may not have thought about the other side of the story. For example, one extremely bright, non-learning disabled sister of a boy with severe learning disabilities began to fail in school. Her parents were very hard on her, insisting that she ought to be able to do the work. At last, this very verbal little girl was able to let them know that they had so carefully avoided praising her effortless achievements and had praised her brother so lavishly for his struggling successes, she felt the only way to be appreciated was to create some problems she could then overcome!

Moving On

Moving on is a stage many people may not reach. When a person feels that those problems he or she has been working through are basically solved, there may be a wish to help others work through the same problems. This is why many people who have adjusted to their disabilities continue to work in organizations for others with disabilities and why many parents whose learning disabled children are grown and successful still

75

continue to work for programs for other LD children, adolescents, adults, and their families.

When I think about parents who have continued to work for the field after their children have grown to adulthood, I always think of the wonderful mother who came to one of my first presentations in Texas. She had just been told that day that her daughter had a learning disability. In shock, she said she had no idea what that meant. She had been told about my presentation that night and had come to my simulation workshop titled "Try a Learning Disability on for Size." This was a program I developed some twenty-five years ago to let parents, teachers, and others experience learning disability as the learning disabled person experiences it. I don't remember meeting her that night, but some years later at a repeat of the workshop, she told me about it. At that time she was president of her local Association for Children with Learning Disabilities. A few years later Lanelle Gallagher was president of the national Learning Disabilities Association with her now-grown, very capable daughter assisting in organizing registration materials for state and national conferences!

Counseling

If you feel that you are having trouble with your learning disability, there is help for you. What kind of help you get depends on what kinds of problems you are having. If your problems are in school or vocational training, you will want to see a counselor who specializes in that area. You might want to skip ahead to Chapter 6, titled "After High School, What?" and Chapter 8, "Jobs: Getting Them and Keeping Them." If your problems have to do with dating or relationships with friends, read Chapter 10, "Love and Relationships." If it's problems with your spouse or your children or the family in general, take a look at Chapter 11, "Marriage and Family."

If, though, you feel that your main problem at this time is coping with this learning disability issue, you might want to consider taking the time to get some counseling right now, just for yourself. You'll want to make a careful choice in the kind of counselor you want to see, depending on your needs and the costs involved. Counseling may range from free to very expensive, and only some kinds may be covered by insurance. Be sure to check carefully so that you know what is involved before you enter into a counseling situation.

Kinds of Counselors

First, there are many different professionals (and non-professionals) who engage in various types of counseling. Some, of course, use terms other than *counseling* for what they do, but I like to use *counseling* as a general term for a helping relationship between a person with a problem and a person with training who assists people with similar problems. Others may refer to it as *therapy* or by some other term. It may be helpful to look at some of the different types of professionals and non-professionals who engage in this work and to study what some of their approaches might be.

1. *Psychiatrist*: A psychiatrist is a medical doctor with a specialization in psychiatry. Psychiatrists deal with a variety of emotional difficulties in varying degrees of severity. Some psychiatrists specialize in psychoanalysis, which explores the background of an individual's emotional development over a long period of time. Psychiatrists, as medical doctors, can also prescribe medication for their patients. For example, if a patient required Ritalin or some other drug for depression, a psychiatrist might prescribe it along with the psychotherapy sessions and would monitor the patient's progress on the drug. Because psychiatrists are medical doctors, some insurance policies cover treatment by a psychiatrist even when such policies do not cover other types of therapy for psychological or emotional problems.

Often a policy may limit the number of visits to a psychiatrist or the amount that will be paid.

2. *Psychologist*: Usually, a psychologist has a PhD degree in psychology. Although properly addressed as Dr. So-and-so, a psychologist is not a medical doctor and cannot prescribe medication. There are many different kinds of psychologists, including several who do not do counseling. Those who do counseling may have a number of different approaches. Behavioral approaches, for example, focus on particular behaviors and what happens before and after them. For example, if every time you fail a test, you eat chocolate, and then you feel better, but later you gain weight, you may be helped to learn to substitute something else for chocolate-eating behavior.

Some psychologists also do psychological and educational testing as well as counseling. In a larger professional setting, trained personnel called *psychometrists* (usually trained by professionals in the field of psychology) or *educational diagnosticians* (usually trained by professionals in the field of education) may do the testing and prepare reports, while psychologists may specialize in counseling. If the setting is medical, the psychologists may also work with a psychiatrist or other medical doctor so that medication may be prescribed when it is needed.

3. *Social worker*: There are also many different kinds of social workers. Some may have master's or doctoral degrees and may have specialized in particular areas of counseling. Some work independently, and others may work in medical or other professional settings. In some clinics, a psychologist or psychiatrist may work with the child or adult client, and a social worker may work with the parents or spouse of the client as a part of the team approach.

4. *Counselor*: The term *counselor* can be a general term for any person who works in a formalized way to help others with problems. This is how I used the term in my introduction to this section, but it can also be a term indicating a person with specific training and a specific role. School counselors, for example, have

training for their role, which includes such areas as vocational counseling as well as helping students with crises and emotional difficulties. There are also *peer counselors*, who are students given some kinds of training to help other students within a school setting. Many churches and synagogues also provide counseling services. Sometimes this service is given by professionals who donate a portion of their time to their local congregations, but often it is provided by lay counselors (non-professionals) who go through training given by those religious institutions. They may or may not be supervised by professionals. Many of these programs are excellent but much depends on the screening of applicants for those positions, on the kind of training they receive, and the kind of supervision provided. With church or synagogue counseling, it is probably best to stay with counselors trained in the denomination closest to your own beliefs or background. There is usually not a charge for this counseling, but it may only be available to members of the congregation offering it.

5. *Therapist*: This is a term that greatly varies in usage. In some states, persons with no training at all can open up shop and call themselves therapists. Many kinds of therapists, such as physical and occupational therapists, have extensive training that is rigorously documented and specified by their professional organizations. The therapists most likely to be seen by learning disabled people may have some designation such as *educational therapist, learning therapist*, or *reading therapist*. It is important to learn about the training and background of such a person. Many can be very helpful and provide useful services, but finding out just what training the individual has had is essential. Some reading therapists, for example, have had training in only one particular approach to reading. In the field of learning disabilities, it is common for specialists in multisensory approaches to have had extensive training in a particular multisensory approach, but in *only* that approach. This means that unless a client's reading problem is one for which that approach is the right one, that therapist will not be able to help. Because many of the

multisensory approaches are thought by their designers to be appropriate for all individuals with reading disabilities, referral to other kinds of assistance may not be made.

A further problem with the term *therapist* is that there are many new therapies that are extremely controversial as always seems to have been the case in the area of learning disabilities. Further, some therapists may be valid practitioners of these new approaches, but others may be untrained individuals simply jumping on the bandwagon. Some of the therapies, no matter how unconventional, may prove to be productive, and others may simply fade away, as have many unusual approaches I have seen in my thirty or more years in the field. Most of the divergent approaches are offered by sincere individuals who believe that their therapies will be useful, and probably very few are out just for the money with no thought of helping. In either case, however, if a person genuinely in need of help wastes time and money on worthless or ineffective approaches, that time and money is lost when it might have gone for valid treatment.

Costs of Counseling

As we have seen, many different kinds of counseling are available, and we should not be surprised at the many different cost levels! Some services can be very expensive, and some are very reasonable, or even provided at no cost. One thing you will want to do is check your insurance policy before you call a counselor. Some companies provide reimbursement for only certain kind of counseling, and some provide it only if you are referred by your doctor. Sometimes only a psychiatrist's services are covered by your policy although, in some cases, psychologists may be covered. Now more and more insurance companies also provide coverage for a variety of licensed counselors, including social workers. Often your policy will limit the amount of reimbursement or the number of visits you may have in a year. It is best to check on this first.

If you are not employed, or if you feel you cannot afford the co-payment portion of your insurance, there are still options open to you. Your city or county health department may offer free or low-cost counseling, either provided by the government agency or by professional volunteers who donate a portion of their time from their professional practices. Your church or synagogue may provide family service counseling. There may be free or low-cost services available through a local college or university. You may find that individual counseling or group counseling is available.

Support Groups

In some areas, support groups for learning disabled people are springing up. For many people, this opportunity to share experiences with other learning disabled people provides the link they need to work through the day-to-day problems that we all face. Most of the groups focus on social activities and information sharing, perhaps including speakers on rights and problems of mutual concern. The groups are often run by learning disabled people like you, so the organization of the group may reflect the kinds of problems many of us have. Some groups may function for a while and then die out when a person who was spearheading the group moves away or feels that his or her problems are solved.

A self-help group that has lasted for a long time is the Marin Puzzle People in California. The group is named for Marin County and for the fact that learning disabled people are often a puzzle to themselves and others! The creativity and resourcefulness of learning disabled people is well represented in the group's annual fund-raiser: The sale of Stay-at-Home tickets for use during the busy holiday season! These tickets, for which donors pay whatever amount they wish to contribute, "entitle" holders to a quiet, peaceful evening at home. Certainly, the season is full of fun, but the hustle and bustle of parties, shopping, and other activities, which is often stressful even to non-learning disabled people, may be very difficult for us to handle. A reminder to take some quiet time out for rest and relaxation may be essential for us as learning disabled adults.

Your local Learning Disability Association (formerly Association for Children with Learning Disabilities) may have a support group. You can call the national organization (listed in the Resources section of this book) for information about your local group. They may be able to direct you to other services as well.

The National Network for Learning Disabled Adults may be able to help you locate a group in your area or you might want to start your own. You will be surprised at the adults of all ages, professionals, students, and workers at a variety of jobs who are interested in such a group. If you are in a college or university setting, the Disabled Student Services Coordinator (or whoever is the campus contact person for disabled students) might be very much interested in starting a group, especially if someone like you is willing to be involved.

Summary

We have looked at some of the stages you may have gone through in confronting your learning disability and some of the sources for help you may want to use. Whether you have known about your learning disability for a long time or have only just found a name for the problems you have had for years, you need to know that you are more than just the sum of your problems. You are a person with abilities, strengths, and goals. You can use your strengths and abilities to work around your disabilities and reach your goals, and it does not lessen your successes to ask for help as you may need it along the way. Others have been successful at achieving fulfilling accomplishments in spite of learning disabilities, and you can, too.

Suggested Reading

Cordoni, Barbara. (1990). *Living with a learning disability* (rev. ed.). Carbondale, IL: Southern Illinois University.
This fine book is written by a woman who established a university program for learning disabled students and who also knows about learning disability through the experiences of two of her four children. The book is chiefly about those persons with learning disabilities that cause social problems although it includes much that is useful to those with more academic problems. An excellent resource section is also included.

East, Joanne. (1987). *Yes you can! A booklet to help young people with learning disabilities understand and help themselves* (rev. ed). Chicago, IL: National Easter Seal Society.
This is a charming booklet, originally conceptualized by a learning disabled fifth grader and her teacher and heavily illustrated in cartoon style by a young man with learning disabilities. Appropriate for upper elementary through adult, this is a good choice as a first introduction to the problem.

Chapter 6

After High School, What?

For many people with learning disabilities, finishing high school is a cross between a relief and a miracle. Some of us declare that we'll *never* place ourselves in a classroom situation again. It may seem that any kind of job is better than having to go to school any more. Some of us might like to try college but aren't sure we can make it. Others have worked for that college opportunity for years, struggling against great difficulty and even harder against people who said there was no chance a learning disabled person could make it in a college setting.

What about dropping out?

Of course, there are different kinds of "finishing" high school. Some student with learning disabilities finish by dropping out. When you're sixteen or seventeen, the kind of job you can get without a high school diploma or special training may look pretty good. For someone still living at home and not paying for rent or groceries or utilities, having enough money to buy clothes, a car, and some entertainment is appealing. At some point, the drive for independence may assert itself, and an apartment and the freedom to make one's own life decisions come next. What to do then?

As many an adult with learning disabilities has found, this may be a turning point. Even young people with learning disabilities who have never been diagnosed or given special help may find themselves facing up to the difficulties of not having enough education or training for a good job. But just because you dropped out at some time in the past does not mean that you have thrown away your chances. There can be many options open to you that you or your teachers and parents were not aware of or that were not available earlier.

College – At Any Age

What if you're a mature person with several years between your last school attendance and the present? Perhaps you are an adult, with children either in school or grown, and you've just discovered that your learning disability was what kept you from succeeding in school. Is it too late for you to think about going to college?

The answer is, absolutely not! This may, in fact, be the perfect time for you to think about advanced education. You're a mature person now with life experience that can help you make realistic, adult decisions about your studies and your goals.

As a college advisor at a woman's university, I often see mature women who either have have no college or perhaps a year or two, who are now considering returning to school. They are often hesitant, worried about their poor academic records in the past, wondering how they can compete with the bright young girls just out of high school. Many of these women feel they are not very bright; some have just discovered that they are learning disabled, and others may find it out along the way. I tell them that in my experience, women like them often make the best students. Why? Because they know how important their studies are, and they are able to put all the extra work they are doing in perspective. Their distractions are family and home responsibilities, not parties and dates, and they are able to find the time to fulfill all their responsibilities, admirably. I tell them, too, that they are likely to be hired first from their graduating class of teachers. What principal wouldn't like to hire a *mature* beginning teacher, who will be paid exactly the same as a young beginner, but who brings extensive life experience and mature judgement to the job?

Often, these women, whom my university calls "returning

students," have been told they're overachievers, and they work under the misapprehension that they are really not able to do all that they are doing. I have always found the label *overachiever* insulting. There is no such thing as an overachiever. If you are able to do the task, that proves you are able to do it. As I often say in my lectures, *overachiever* is a label used by people who won't admit they were wrong about something. If a bucket holds more than you thought it would, it's just a bigger bucket than you thought. Likewise, if a person achieves more than you thought possible, it simply means your expectations were too low.

So if college looks like an exciting possibility, don't let your age or your academic past have too much influence on you decision. Even if you had a very bad experience in college some years ago and failed, look into the possibility of giving it another try. In some cases, colleges can overlook or erase some early records of students returning to school after an absence of several years, depending on the circumstances.

The GED and College

If you are interested in college training, you may find that most colleges require you to have finished high school. Some will permit entry to those who can achieve a certain score on a standardized test. You may, of course, request special accommodations for testing. (These are discussed later in this chapter.)

You may want to explore returning to night school to finish your high school education whether or not you decide to go on to college. You may take classes one or two at a time, usually in the evenings, and pass some exams. Luckily, the classes are often small and include many adults like yourself. You'll almost certainly see some people older than yourself, and you may see a number of other learning disabled people. You will probably find that a few of them are finding out for the first time that they have learning disabilities.

You may prefer to obtain a certificate of high school equivalency, which is what the substitute for a high school diploma is called. The most widely known is the GED, or General Educational Development tests. You may take the test under special conditions, such as extended time, or with a scribe to record your answers, if you request these accommodations and can document the need. For information on the GED and other equivalency programs, write for the brochure "High School Diploma Alternatives" prepared by HEATH Resource Center. It is listed in the Resources section at the end of this chapter.

To find out more about high school equivalency classes and tests in your area, call your school district office. They can give you the information and help you find classes in your area.

Facts About Colleges and Universities

If college is your choice, you may find that you are in the luckiest generation of LD people ever. Though college is not necessarily easy for anyone, special assistance for learning disabled students in colleges and universities is more available now than it has ever been. In the past, college was a sink-or-swim proposition. The student had to muddle through alone, and only the best students survived. Even many non-learning disabled students had trouble making the grade. For some of them, of course, the problem was that school had never been hard for them, and they didn't know how to study. That's certainly not your situation: You *know* it's going to be hard, so you will want to be prepared. You already know that you are going to have to study harder than most people, but there are some other things that can help you, too.

Admissions Requirements

Requirements vary from one college or university to another, and it is important to find out ahead of time what the requirements are. Because Section 504 of the Rehabilitation Act of 1973 requires that a qualified handicapped student can't be excluded from programs that receive federal aid, certain requirements may be waived or modified in some way. If you are still in high school, your school counselor will have most of the information you need about the requirements of a particular college. If not, college catalogs are available by calling or writing to the college to request one. Also, you will find summaries of requirements in some of the guides to college for students with learning disabilities listed in the Resources section of this book.

Community Colleges

Most community colleges have very liberal admission standards, requiring only that you either have completed high school or have the equivalency certificate. You may not be eligible to take some courses that transfer to four-year colleges or universities until you have completed some basic or remedial courses. Generally, the community colleges have been the leaders in providing special services for students with learning disabilities. They also have the advantage of their location in your home community, so that living expenses are not an issue, and of low tuition costs in comparison to four-year schools. Instructors tend to be hired for their ability to teach rather than for the kinds of research and publication skills in which universities may be more interested.

Four-Year Colleges and Universities

Four-year colleges or universities have more stringent requirements for admission than do community colleges. They may require admissions testing and a certain grade-point average in high school. Many private colleges and some major universities require ranking within a certain percentage of your high school class and a personal interview for admission. A student with learning disabilities may be required to show that he or she has alternative means of coping with the disability in the college setting.

Admissions Testing

Usually, colleges do require that an admissions test be taken even though they may adjust the requirements for a certain level of performance. The ACT or SAT test is typically required, but the law ensures that you may take these tests under non-standard conditions if it is necessary because of your learning disability. It is important to request non-standard conditions well in advance of the time you will be taking the test. This is because additional space or personnel may be required for your testing. If, for example, you request additional time, arrangements will need to be made for an examiner to be available to supervise you during the time needed. Some non-standard conditions you may request are:

Additional time for testing
A separate room to reduce distraction
Use of cassette recorder or a reader
A large-print version of the test

Whether or not an admissions interview is required at the school in which you are interested, it may be helpful for you to request one. If only a few universities offer the program you want to pursue, and your qualifications aren't quite up to their requirements, an interview may help you convince the admissions officer that you are willing to put in the time and effort necessary to be successful. It will also give you a chance to see what modifications or accommodations might be possible. If you do get an interview, go well prepared. Know exactly what the catalog says about the program in which you are interested and be prepared to show how you plan to overcome any obstacles. Going for an interview will also give you an opportunity to visit the campus.

Choosing a College

As you consider the requirements of a college or university you might want to attend, remember to keep in mind your particular handicaps, your goals, and the accommodations you may need to reach your goals. Trying to by-pass admissions requirements may not be a good idea if it means that you will not receive the special assistance you may need. The services a college or university is able to provide you may be among the major factors that can help you succeed.

What special services do learning disabled students need?

For most students, picking a college is a matter of looking at what they want to study and what they can afford. For you, there is at least one other consideration that is just as important as these two, and that's whether or not the college or university is prepared to give you the kind of help and support services you may need.

Learning disabled students need different kinds of services, depending on their specific disabilities. It will be important to match your needs to the services provided by your school. In the book *Unlocking Potential*, which I recommend highly, Barbara Scheiber and Jeanne Talpers divide the levels of support learning disabled students receive into the following three levels:

1. The first level is *minimal support*. At this level, you as a student will be the one who is doing the adapting. You generally will find that some schools provide very little in the way of extra services, perhaps just enough to meet federal regulations. Any

services, such as academic advising and study centers, are likely to be available to all students and may not be adapted to suit your needs. For some learning disabled students, this level of support might be adequate. Such a student would be one who has developed a good background of adaptations, and knows, for example, that he or she might need to take light course loads in order to succeed or to purchase textbooks in advance of a given semester in order to start reading ahead of time. Independence and good social skills may also be necessary for a student who will be receiving only minimal support from the institution.

2. At the *moderate support* level, services exist on the campus to help you make the adjustments necessary to be successful. There may be a special office or individual available to assist you as well as additional tutorial or support services, including intervention with faculty in cases when some advocacy is needed. It is helpful if there has also been faculty training in modifying course requirements to meet the needs of students with learning disabilities. I have worked with several colleges and universities in providing in-service training not only for all faculty members, but, in one or two notable cases, the upper administration, including the college or university president, vice president, and deans. Generally, the focus of moderate support is helping the student adjust, but the student will be expected to ask for help and to know when it is needed.

3. For some students, only a campus with *intensive support* might be appropriate. On such a campus, the focus is on adapting the program and services to your needs as a learning disabled student rather than helping you to adapt to existing programs. In most cases, these colleges and universities welcome learning disabled students and make it a point to advertise their programs and services. Schreiner College in the Texas hill country, for example, expects that as their special program grows, as many as one fourth of their enrollment may be learning disabled students taking advantage of their trained faculty and large community-

volunteer tutor corps. Landmark College in Vermont is nationally known as a program well-geared to the needs of students with learning disabilities. You should be aware, however, that these highly specialized colleges can be quite expensive.

What level of support do you need?

To select a college that is right for you, you will want to consider your particular needs. If minimal support is right for you, and you are able to adjust to the college setting on your own, then you need only consider admissions requirements and costs for any college or university that offers the programs you wish to study, where you want to study them.

If you will need more than minimal support in your program, a number of directories, updated every year or so, can give you information on the kinds of programs, special services, and general requirements of a large number of schools serving learning disabled students. Check your public library or bookstore for one of the guides to college for learning disabled students recommended in the Resource section at the end of this chapter.

You should consider, though, that simply selecting a college because it offers extensive services for students with learning disabilities may not be a good idea if many of those services are things you do not need. If you have difficulty deciding exactly how much support you may need, it may be time to look at your most recent educational assessment with an expert. Both your academic patterns and the pattern of your social strengths and weaknesses will be important in determining what will be needed to make your college experience successful and rewarding.

Making a Campus Visit

After you have done some checking on colleges or universities that look like good possibilities for you, nothing can take the place of a visits to the campus, preferable while classes are in session.

Many colleges and universities have planned Preview Week sessions during which you (and your parents, if that's appropriate) can visit the campus, stay in the dormitory, sit in on classes, and talk to advisors. These are excellent opportunities to get a good feel for the campus atmosphere. If no preview sessions are available, ask the admissions officer to set up a visit schedule for you and indicate in advance the programs you'd like to visit. As an advisor, I frequently see prospective students making a campus visit who just drop in without appointments, often from many miles away. They are just as frustrated as I when we are unable to set up appointments on the spot with people they need to see.

You will want to get the feel of the campus environment and programs in a way that you cannot by reading about them, calling on the telephone, or briefly visiting during a vacation period. Whether you favor a small college in a rural town, a college or university in a more urban setting, or one of the mega-universities, your choice should depend on the kind of setting in which you think you will be comfortable. Sometimes an unhurried visit can tell you in ways no advisor can whether a particular campus is a good match for you.

As we have already discussed, there are many different kinds of learning disabilities and many different combinations of accommodations that might be necessary to help a particular student achieve. The particular student we're concerned with is *you*, so it will be important for you to examine the services offered in light of your own needs. No matter how elaborate a set-up a college or university offers, if it does not include a critical feature you need, and if the program is hesitant to provide that feature, it may not be the appropriate setting for you.

It is important, too, to find out if the kinds of special services you may need are available as a part of your regular tuition or if there is an additional charge for special services. Some colleges charge a per-semester flat fee for extra services with no limit on the number of services or hours of services, and others charge according to the services you need. You will want to balance the cost against the benefits available.

Adaptations and Modifications

Let's look at some of the adaptations that may make college programs accessible for students with learning disabilities.

1. *Light loads*: Some students may have disabilities so mild that taking light loads each semester – that is, taking only half or three-fourths as many classes as other students – may be the only adjustment necessary. Of course, that means that it may take twice as long to finish a program as it would if you took full course loads. One important thing to remember, though, is that after you have completed your program, nobody ever asks how long it took. The date your degree was granted or your course of study was completed, as well as how well you did, is what is wanted. Sometimes your grades are not critical either so long as you meet graduation requirements, and the only thing that matters is whether or not you finished the program successfully. Most often, however, your grades *do* make a difference. I have often advised a student to drop a course that she was in danger of failing and to re-take it the following semester to protect her grade point average. The more courses you complete with low grades, the harder it is to pull up your average later. Staying in close touch with a good advisor during the term is essential.

Sometimes, a particular scholarship or financial aid program will require that a student be enrolled for a minimum number of semester hours or courses. Also, in some cases, a student must be enrolled full-time to be eligible for some of the special services for disabled students. Find out what the requirements are so that you will not risk eligibility for those funds or special services. Usually, the requirement is that a student take the equivalent of three or four courses to be considered a full-time student. Average course loads may be five courses, and able students may be able to get special permission to take up to seven courses. That's something you probably will not want to attempt.

A student with learning disabilities who is just beginning college should probably enroll for only three or four courses. That will give the student a chance to work out study schedules and determine what extra help or accommodations may be needed.

Even if you think the only accommodation you will need is enrollment for light course loads, look closely at what other services are available on the campus you are considering. You may need some other services or advice later, and you will want to know in advance if it is available.

2. *Study skills courses; remedial courses:* Many colleges and universities offer special study skills courses that can help students learn the skills necessary to approach their courses in an organized, effective way. Notetaking, routine study, how to study for exams, learning to prepare term papers – a variety of special skills may be taught. Other courses that may be helpful include special remedial courses in specific subjects, such as math or English or reading. In some cases, you may be required to take a remedial course if you have not made a certain score on a test in that area of study. Check with your advisor about these courses. While they may be extremely helpful, they frequently do not count for academic credit towards your degree and may affect any financial aid you may receive.

3. *Disabled student services offices:* One of the most helpful accommodations for college students with learning disabilities is a centralized office on campus that provides services for disabled students. Services may range from minimal to extensive. Because of federal law, most colleges and universities now have a designated individual within the administration or staff who is in charge of issues related to disabled students. When considering a particular college or university, find out who that individual is and make a point of talking to him or her. There are several things you will want to know.

You'll want to find out if the individual in charge is hired full-time for disabled student services or has other responsibilities. Unfortunately, in some cases, the person in charge really is that in name only and has so many other responsibilities that there is no help available to disabled students. Luckily, this is changing, and more and more universities and colleges are recognizing the importance of a full-time coordinator of services for disabled students.

If you will require more than slight assistance, you would be best served by someone whose job it is to work with learning disabled students exclusively, but not all colleges or universities are large enough to provide that luxury. More often, there may be a coordinator of disabled student services whose job it is to be sure that *all* students with disabilities find appropriate accommodations on the campus. These duties may range from making sure that construction on the campus doesn't present physical barriers to physically handicapped or blind students all the way to providing direct tutorial services to students with learning disabilities. At a larger school, the coordinator will have others working with and for him or her to provide those services.

At the college or university you are considering, ask the coordinator of disabled student services specifically what is provided and compare that array with the services you will need. Again, nothing can take the place of meeting with the coordinator personally. You can tell a great deal about the willingness of the college or university to assist you by the way in which the coordinator responds to your questions. If there are questions that a general advisor was not able to answer for you, such as questions about alternative ways of satisfying admissions standards or graduation requirements, the disabled student services coordinator should be able to help you.

One very important service that should be provided by a disabled student services coordinator is liaison with faculty. Usually, a student with a disability may register with the disabled student services office, document his or her disability, and request a letter that the student may hand-carry to instructors, a letter that requests certain types of accommodation in the classroom. The student is free to use the letter or not, depending on the circumstances. The letter lets the faculty member know exactly what accommodations are considered appropriate, and also that the requests are valid. Accommodations that might be requested from an individual instructor might include:

- reserved preferential seating in the classroom
- extended time for tests, or testing in the learning center
- oral testing
- additional time for class projects or term papers
- alternative forms for required papers or projects
- copies of charts or other material used in overhead projection during lecture
- permission to tape lectures
- individual assistance

Ask the coordinator to arrange for you to meet and talk with other students with learning disabilities on campus. There should be some means for learning disabled students to be in contact with one another. Often the student grapevine can provide invaluable information about professors who are particularly helpful – or those who tend not to be accommodating to learning disabled students.

Be sure to ask the coordinator about his or her experiences with the department in which you plan to study. If you hope to study social work, for example, and you learn that the social work department at the school you are considering has a record of offering help and support to students with learning disabilities, this information can make your choice of a college that much easier. Of course, finding that your chosen department is the only one on campus that is *not* very accommodating can also make your choice easier although not in the way you would have hoped.

4. *Notetakers and scribes:* For students who have severe writing problems, either in penmanship or in getting complete ideas down on paper, or who have trouble changing information they receive through their ears into written material, notetakers can be a wonderful help. A notetaker attends classes with the learning disabled student and takes notes during the lecture and class discussions. The learning disabled student then is free to focus on the class presentation but later has written notes to use in study. Notetakers do not attend class *for* the student, but *with* the student. Usually they receive some training in notetaking and are paid by funding through the disabled student services office. Even though the notetaker may have had training, some discussion with the student may help clarify the kinds of information the notes should contain and the form that would be most helpful.

When notetakers are not available, some students with learning disabilities enlist the aid of another student in a particular class to share notes. This can be done using carbon sets, special notetaking paper that makes an original for the volunteer notetaker with a copy to give away. More commonly now, the volunteer notetaker simply allows the other student to make a photocopy of the notes. With a coin- or card-operated copy machine in just about every class building on a college campus, this is often a practical solution. Problems may include not being able to find a volunteer who is a good notetaker himself or herself, absences of the notetaker, or inability to find someone willing to help out in this way.

A *scribe* is different from a notetaker in that a scribe may work for the student with learning disabilities during examinations or in working on class papers. An examination scribe writes the answers to essay or short discussion questions for the student, but only as the student dictates those answers. Usually, scribes are instructed not to ask questions or to make comments other than to control the speed of dictation. The scribe's job is only to serve as the writing hands of the student, not to add to or to clarify the answers.

A scribe may also work for a learning disabled student in preparing term papers or other written assignments. Again, the work is designed, sequenced, and dictated by the student. It is not the scribe's job to do the intellectual or scholarly portion of the work, but to serve as the vehicle for transmitting that information to paper. The degree to which the scribe is allowed to serve as an editor may vary from one school to another and even from one instructor to another. Some instructors may resist permitting learning disabled students to use scribes unless assured that the scribe will only transcribe exactly what the student dictates.

The scribe may also serve as the typist, or that may be done by someone else, just as a non-learning disabled student may hire someone to type a term paper. Who pays for the typing varies from one institution to another. In most cases, however, the expense is considered that of the student in the same manner as non-learning disabled students pay for their own typing.

5. *Readers:* For learning disabled students with a reading problem, just working through the world of written material required in the average college class is a problem. Many schools provide paid or volunteer readers who will read text and supplemental material to dyslexic students.

6. *Taped textbooks and/or lectures:* Taped textbooks may be available through services for blind or print-impaired (another term for *dyslexic*) students. Usually, there is a delay when a new text or new edition of a text is selected for a course, and it may be necessary to have a text taped a chapter at a time or to use a reader until a tape is available. Find out if the college you are considering has a system for making taped texts available or if you must make your own arrangements.

Relatively few colleges or universities provide lecture tapes. Whether a lecture tape is prepared by the university's audiovisual department or made by the student, it is important to remember that a two-hour lecture takes two hours to listen to later on tape – or even longer if the student stops the tape from time to time to make notes. Simply accumulating a stack of lecture tapes will not be helpful if there is not time to utilize them.

7. *Class outlines:* Some colleges and universities require instructors in basic courses to provide outlines for each day's lectures so that all students, not just learning disabled students, know the structure of what will be covered that day. This makes notetaking easier, with the basic material already in print so that the student need only to add details.

8. *Alternative testing:* Various forms of alternative testing should be available for learning disabled students. In some cases, all that may be necessary is additional time to complete an examination. If the classroom is scheduled for another class in the hour immediately following, some instructors will allow learning disabled students to arrive early or to complete the test in the instructor's office. Other adaptations, such as a reader or scribe, may require that another test site be used so that other students taking the exam are not distracted. Often a campus will have a learning center whose staff can be contacted by a professor and arrangements made for the student to be tested at that location, either at the same time that the other students are being tested, or at another time. The learning center staff can be given special instructions from the professor, such as whether or not a dictionary may be used, or if staff may paraphrase questions if needed.

9. *Tutorial centers; tutors:* A tutorial center may have any of several different names. *Learning Center, Learning Assistance Center, Study Skills Center,* and *Student Assistance Center* are some of the names commonly used. In some cases, these centers provide special study skills classes and assistance for any student who asks. In other cases, the centers are for handicapped students only. They may be staffed with one or more professionals, and perhaps trained readers, interpreters for the deaf, and tutors. Sometimes the readers, interpreters, or tutors are volunteers, either other students or community volunteers.

10. *Student support groups:* More and more frequently, support groups for handicapped students are appearing on college

and university campuses. Sometimes there is a group for students will all disabilities; sometimes there are several different groups. My university has both an organization for disabled students in general and an older group, SOLD, Support Organization for Learning Disabilities, which includes learning disabled students, learning disabled faculty, and other students and faculty interested in supporting the group. This organization holds typical support meetings with brown-bag luncheons and gripe sessions, but it has also been instrumental in faculty awareness by participating in faculty development programs on learning disabilities and preparing a videotape featuring successful learning disabled students discussing their problems and triumphs.

11. *Tape recorders, calculators, electronic spellers, word processors,* and *computers:* Usually, students are responsible for providing their own small electronics, such as recorders, calculators, and spellers. Some colleges and universities provide computer labs where students can sign up for computer time for preparation of class papers and term projects. Use of these as class aids is now widely accepted, but it is still important to follow proper etiquette for using such aids. Students should always ask permission before taping lectures or other programs. I permit taping only by students who ask in advance because I want to be aware that my words may be heard not only by those present, but also by others. I also request that the tape be erased after the student completes the course. I do not permit taping of an exam review class because all the material covered at that time should be included in earlier tapes or notes.

If you are dysgraphic but can produce acceptable written text with a lap-top word processor or computer, find out if you will be permitted to use it in class, either for notetaking or examinations. Because modern machines are very quiet except during printing, there should be no objection to your using this mode for class work with printing done later. Many, if not most, machines now include such options as spelling and grammar checkers as well as built-in thesaurus programs. For this reason, use of the machines in writing classes in which spelling or grammar is part of the curriculum may be limited. Be sure to check with the instructor.

12. *Special advisory assistance:* Make a point of going to the department in which you intend to study. Ask to talk to an advisor in that department about the sequence of courses. In some departments, especially at larger universities or in large programs, there will be one advisor just for freshman students who transfer credits from community colleges or other universities. Very few will have advisors who work specifically with learning disabled students. For most learning disabled students, it may be best to have one advisor who works with you throughout your program. In any case, it will be essential for you to maintain regular contact with the appropriate advisor.

If the specialty you will be studying is one in which there are certain requirements with which you will need assistance, you will want to know the department's flexibility and willingness to work with the disabled students' coordinator and with you.

13. *Counseling:* Some of the problems learning disabled students face in the college setting may be the same as those of other students; some may be directly related to the learning disability itself. Most colleges and universities have counseling departments where students can get assistance with personal problems as a part of the regular services of the school. It might be helpful to ask if the college or university you are considering has counselors who are experienced in working with learning disabled students if you think you may need such services.

A problem many learning disabled students have is knowing when to ask for help. It is easier to seek assistance if you know in advance whom to call. Often it is too easy to put off asking for help when you know that you will have to make several calls to find out whom you need to talk to. Whether it is personal counseling or academic assistance, getting all the telephone number and all the basic information about available services long before you think you may need them is the best idea.

Summary

The opportunity to attend college, once thought out of reach for students with learning disabilities of more than the mildest nature, is now a very real possibility. The courts have insisted that this educational opportunity be available even if modifications and adjustment must be made. An array of services is becoming more and more common in colleges and universities, making it possible for the student with learning disabilities to select those accommodations necessary to ensure success. And, just as the special modifications appropriate for handicapped children and teens taught educators techniques that were useful for *all* learners, college and university teachers and administrators are finding that techniques for college students with learning disabilities are often good techniques for all college students. It was gratifying but not surprising to find, after I had completed a faculty awareness workshop for a small college, that those faculty members who had been the most receptive and who had asked the most insightful questions were featured in a booklet about their college as individuals who had won awards as outstanding teachers. The kind of personal attention that goes into providing assistance to students with learning disabilities is the kind of personal attention that helps other students succeed as well.

If your career goals involve the need for college education, begin exploring programs in your chosen field as early as you can. Whether you feel that a program in a two-year community college or a university degree program is right for you or whether you'd just like to take a few personal development courses without a specific program of study, college may be not just a possibility for you, it may be a definite probability.

Suggested Resources

High School Equivalency

HEATH Resource Center. (1991). *High School Diploma Alternatives*. Washington, DC: Author
This single-page bulletin gives information on a variety of ways adults may obtain high school credit, either by diploma or examination. Addresses and telephone numbers are included.

Your Rights as a College Student with Learning Disabilities

Association on Higher Education and Disability. (undated). *Section 504: The law and its impact*. Columbus, OH: Author.
This little brochure available from AHEAD (formerly AHSSPPE) describes your rights as a college student with learning disabilities under Section 504. It's handy to have and to show to others who have questions about the law.

Succeeding in College with Learning Disabilities

Griggs, Mary Jo, & Wiar, Ceceila M. (1986). *Living with a learning disability: A handbook for high school and college students*. Waterford, MI: Minerva Press.
This brief handbook includes background on learning disabilities and listing of suggestions for academic and social situations. Resources are also listed.
HEATH Resource Center. (undated). *Ready, set, go!!!: Helping LD students prepare for college*. Washington, DC: Author.
This pamphlet from HEATH will be helpful for students,

parents, or counselors. It contains 20 suggestions for helping prepare for the transition to college.

Scheiber, Barbara, & Talpers, Jeanne (1987). *Unlocking potential: College and other choices for learning disabled people, A step-by-step guide.*
This outstanding book has been recommended earlier. In addition to the first chapter, which is a fine introduction to learning disabilities, the book describes procedures for acquiring college or vocational training. A very useful feature is the inclusion of more than twenty lists, charts, or graphs that summarize some of the important information given.

Vogel, Susan A. (1990). *College students with learning disabilities: A handbook* (3rd ed). Pittsburgh, PA: Learning Disabilities Association.
This small book is useful for college students with disabilities as well as for admissions personnel, faculty, and college administrators. Appendices include a list of U.S. Department of Education Regional Civil Rights Offices, organizations, and a variety of sources of information.

Wren, Carol, & Segal, Laura. (1985). *College students with learning disabilities.* Chicago, IL: Depaul University.
Laura's own story as a learning disabled college student is told in this booklet. Information about learning disability, the diagnostic process, and accommodations for college student is alternated with personal experiences.

Information About Special Testing for College Admission

American College Test (ACT): For an information brochure including the application for special testing arrangements, write to:

Admissions Testing Program
ATP Services for Handicapped Students
P.O. Box 6226
Princeton, NJ 08541-6226
or call (609) 921-9000

Scholastic Aptitude Test (SAT): A packet containing information on the two types of non-standard testing available (Plan A, special accommodations, and Plan B, extended time only) and an application is available from:

ACT Test Administration
Special Testing P.O. Box 168
Iowa City, IA 52243
or telephone (319) 337-1332

Guides

Many of the guides available are updated frequently, but even then, information may be out of date as colleges and universities change programs. Although it may be helpful to consider a college based on information in the guides, be sure to check that the services are still available before making a final decision.

Jarrow, J., Baker, B., Hartman, R., Harris, R. Lesh, K., Redden, M., & Smithson, J. (1986). *How to choose a college: Guide for the student with a disability.*Columbus, OH: Association of Handicapped Student Service Programs in Postsecondary Education (AHSSPPE) and Higher Education and the Handicapped (HEATH).

Lipkin, Midge. (date unknown). *The schoolsearch guide to colleges with programs and services for students with learning disabilities.* Belmont, MA: Schoolsearch.

Liscio, M.A. (1984). *A guide to colleges for learning disabled students.* Orlando, FL: Academic Press.

Mangrum, C.T., II, & Strichart, S.S. (1984). *College and the learning disabled student: A guide to program selection, development, and implementation.* Orlando, FL: Grune & Stratton.

Mangrum, C.T., II, & Strichart S.S. (1988) *Peterson's colleges with programs for learning-disabled students* (2nd Ed.). Princeton, NJ: Peterson's Guides.

Scheiber, B., & Talpers, J. (1985). *Campus access for learning disabled students: A comprehensive guide.* Washington, DC: Closer Look.

Slovak, I. (1984). *BOSC directory of facilities for learning disabled people.* Congers, NY: BOSC.

Straughn, C.T., & Colby, S.C. (1985). *Lovejoy's college guide for the learning disabled.* New York: Monarch.

Chapter 7

Around the House

Whether you live alone, with your parents, or with your spouse, there are some aspects of home life that may be difficult for people with learning disabilities. Left to our natural state, most of us are not very well organized people. Yet we are often resistant to change, so that if someone tries to help us by tidying up after us, it may upset us unreasonably!

Some of us have learned on our own to develop ways of being organized that help us keep ahead of the clutter and disorganization. Sometimes our methods work for a while, but then let us down or end up being more work than doing it another way.

I remember a few years ago when the columnist Heloise wrote that she couldn't stand the untidy look of an unmade bed, and she hated making it first thing in the morning. So she developed a way of making it up while she was still in it, and then sliding out carefully from under the covers, needing then only to flip up the top of the spread over the pillow and give it a pat! That always seemed to me so awkward that it might be more work than it was worth – but if it worked for her, then it was a good method – *for her*.

I hate an unmade bed, too, but I know if I walk away from it, I'll never get back to it, and it'll nag me until I leave the house and upset me when I get home. So I make mine as soon as I get up – even before my eyes are fully open. Of course, I have planned ahead. I use a heavy quilted spread, almost like a comforter, which hides wrinkles underneath if I have not been too tidy. I think that's close enough. Some people just use one of those comforters as both a blanket and a spread because it hides all sorts of wrinkled sheets underneath. Then they use matching pillowcases on their pillows. They only have to pull the comforter over the sheets, plop the pillows on top, and in 15 seconds it looks almost as good as a fancy bedspread with matching pillow shams.

I use other tricks to eliminate jobs I really don't like to do, but which, left undone, would lead to results that would bother me. I hate to scrub my glass shower door, but I would also hate to see it all water-spotted and grubby looking. So after every shower, I spend ten seconds wiping the door with an old towel I keep handy for that purpose. (Really just two quick passes down each door!) My ten-year-old shower door (which I installed myself) still looks new, and I have never had to do a serious scrubbing on it.

Deciding What Household Tasks Need to Be Done

There are so many household tasks that seem to need doing! If I kept my house as clean as my mother insisted on keeping ours when I was growing up, I would have to give up my job or any social life I might like to have. For years, I struggled with that. I tried to keep things spotless and in order and felt guilty when I just couldn't vacuum twice a week or scrub and wax the kitchen floor every week.

Finally, I realized that it was just not realistic for me to set such a standard for myself and that many other busy professional people had also come to the same conclusion. I tried to look at the household jobs that bothered me if they weren't done and worry only about them. The others I just decided not to trouble myself with until they got to a level I couldn't stand.

If you live alone, or have a private area of the dwelling place you share with others, you might be able to use my approach, figuring out which housekeeping chores come first and which can wait. If you live with a spouse or roommate, you will want to work this out together. If you live at home with your parents, this may take some negotiating because different generations have different standards for household tasks. If my mother were coming for a visit, for example, I would finally have to do all of those cleaning jobs I had been putting off!

I suggest you start by making two lists. One list should include all the things around the house that bother you if they're not done. The other list should include things you think *ought* to be taken care of but that don't bother you very much.

If you live with a spouse or roommate, make your lists separately, and then you can compare them later. Your list might not look very much like mine, but here's the way mine goes:

Things that really bother me to live with:

unmade bed
sticky kitchen floor
stacks of newspapers
dirty toilets
spots on shower door
dirty bathtub and sink
stuff stacked on bed
bugs in house
unmowed lawn
smelly garbage in house
dirty laundry stacking up
inside of car dirty
cat litter pan needs changing
towels not hung up neatly

Things that don't bother me too much:

stacks of books all over the house
stacks of paperwork here and there
dust on mini-blinds
little baskets full of miscellaneous items all over house
clothes on hangers hanging on door
dirty dishes in kitchen (as long as they are rinsed and in sink,

not on counter)
unironed clean laundry stacking up
untidy closets (with the door closed to hide the mess)
untidy kitchen cabinets (also with the doors closed)
outside of car dirty
cat hair on couch

Just making the list is helpful. As you think about what really
bothers you and what does not, you may find that you have been
spending too much time on the things that make little difference
to you whether they are done or not. If that's the case, you can
easily see some changes you might want to make.

For example, I hate putting away clean dishes out of the
dishwasher, so I don't do it until I have a sink full of dirties to put
in (or company is coming). Luckily, as long as the dirty dishes are
rinsed and ready to go in the dishwasher, I don't mind them too
much as long as they're not on the counter but are neatly stacked
in the sink. Of course, if I shared my home with someone who
really hated dirty dishes in the sink, that might present a problem
we would have to negotiate. If that person weren't a neat towel-
hanger-upper, maybe we could work out a deal.

Now that you have your lists, look at each item on the "really
bothers me" list. Decide how often you need to do the jobs and
work out your schedule. Then check your "doesn't bother me too
much" list for things that might provide a health hazard if left
undone. Unpleasant as it may be, those need to be moved to the
other lists so that you can get them done as well.

Working with a Spouse or Roommate

If you live with a spouse or roommate, compare your lists and
make one new one. On the "really bothers us" side, put all of the
things you both agreed on. Later, you can divide up the tasks.

Next, list each item you both agreed belong on your "doesn't
bother us too much" list. These may have to wait as long as they

aren't items that could cause health problems if left too long!

Now examine what you have left. If an unmade bed bothers one spouse but not the other, then perhaps making the bed should be assigned to the one who's bothered if it isn't made. If roommates have separate rooms, closing a door to a bedroom can solve the unmade bed problem and a lot of others!

Look at all your areas of conflict and try to resolve them through deciding that the partner most bothered by the problem will be the one charged with doing something about it. The areas that will be difficult are those in which the particular mess is the responsibility of one partner who doesn't find it a problem, but which bothers the other! For example, if the cat belongs to one partner, but the odor from the litter box bothers the other, then clearly the cat owner needs to take care of it. Perhaps the one who isn't the cat's owner can agree to point out when the litter needs changing or make sure that fresh cat litter is on the shopping list.

Let's look at some common "around the house" problem areas and some ideas for solutions.

Grocery Shopping

A common problem is forgetting to purchase something you need. Obviously, making a list is at least part of the answer, but with our LD memory problems, sitting down and making the list requires a lot of organization. One good idea is to keep a running list. As soon as you notice that you are low on eggs, write "eggs" on a list that you keep somewhere handy, perhaps on the door of the refrigerator, with a pencil on a string attached to it.

My daughter uses one of those dry-erase boards for a variety of things: telephone messages for family members, reminders, groceries, and so forth. I love the idea for messages, but not for a grocery list since you can't very well take the board down and take it with you to the store, and re-copying it would be a pain in the neck for me. I like to use something I can keep track of and take to the store with me.

I use a 4" x 6" card for my grocery list, and I write things on it in groups according to where they are in the grocery store that I use most of the time. My list may look pretty strange when there are only one or two things on it because I may have written "lettuce" on the left side at the bottom and "peanut butter" over on the right about halfway up, but as I fill it in, it keeps me from missing something that I might put on my list but overlook when I get to the store. If I see that I will run out of onions tomorrow, I will put it after "lettuce" since they're in the same section of the grocery store, and so forth.

Some people find it helpful to cross off or check each item as they put it in the grocery basket. I don't find that I need to do this. One thing I have to do, though, is remember to *throw the list away* when I am finished. Otherwise, I may come across it later, not realize that it isn't a current list, and confuse myself.

I have also found a problem I have with lists that working on this book has helped me solve. Because I *am* a list-maker, I make them constantly. I have already mentioned that I have had to train myself to throw the list away once I have taken care of the items on it. Another problem, though, is making lists on the back of other lists or on the back of some other piece of paper I need to keep! I think I need to make myself a new rule: Write notes on new notepapers only. Perhaps it's time to buy a new pack of 4" x 6" cards.

The only way to be sure you'll have what you need in the house is to write it down as soon as you know you need it. That means everyone has to agree to use the lists and then to do it!

Cooking

I love to cook, but I hate to clean the kitchen. The only time I really enjoy kitchen duty these days is when I visit my daughter. She lets me cook all I want, and she follows me around and cleans up the mess. She is a much better organized cook than I, but insists she doesn't mind tidying up after me.

114

There are probably three major problems that people with learning disabilities have in cooking: first, having all the items needed for a particular dish or meal on hand; second, getting the sequence of steps in the correct order without forgetting a step or ingredient; third, planning properly so that all the items for a meal are ready at the right time.

Planning ahead and list-making are useful techniques for cooking tasks. If you've used your list-making well in shopping for groceries, you can be sure of having everything on hand before you start to cook.

Next, figure out what you're going to do, step by step. If you plan to have salad, you will want to make it ahead of time and store it in the refrigerator if the main dish is one that will take constant attention. If the main dish is a casserole or something that will cook pretty much on its own after you get it started, you might want to make the salad while the main dish is cooking or baking.

One friend lists all the major steps in evening meal-planning with a wipe-off marker on the backsplash area behind her stove. Whether it is for a family meal or a big dinner party (and I have been at her home when she served 15 or 18 people!), the list keeps her on track. She can then check off each item as it is done. By planning to prepare some items the day before, she always seems naturally well-organized. She confesses that without her list, however, she would never make it.

It would take many pages of this book to discuss all the aspects of cooking that you might want to work out with your learning disability in mind. That is more than is intended here. As you have read the earlier chapters and learned more about your particular learning problems and strengths, perhaps you can work out your own strategies for making cooking one of your skills.

If you find you're not a very good cook without a recipe to follow, and you have trouble figuring out what items go together to make a balanced, attractive meal, you might want to look at some of the newer convenience cookbooks. Many are organized around entire meals with all the steps coordinated and listed for you.

Of course, kitchen safety is critical, too. My memory problems have caused many a kitchen blunder. I often say that my recipe for cooking frozen peas is: "Place peas and water in pot. Turn on heat. When it boils over, peas are done!" I have also been known to leave a stove burner turned on for a long time after I have removed a pot. Because I know that this is a problem for me, I make it a rule to check the stove before leaving the house or going to bed at night. I would be embarrassed to report how often I have to turn something off!

As you might imagine, keeping a kitchen fire extinguisher in an accessible place is important, too. Of course, smoke alarms in working order, with the batteries checked often, are important for the whole house or apartment, not just for the kitchen.

There are other safety issues in the kitchen as well. To avoid burns from my clumsiness, I am careful to keep pot handles turned away so that I am less likely to knock something over. I also am careful about knives and other sharp objects. I keep all knives in a separate place, and I never leave a knife in a sink full of water.

Sales and Coupons

Shopping sales and using cents-off coupons can represent a big savings in the budget. Often, though, learning disabled people feel they are not well enough organized to keep up with coupons or sales or that they are just too busy coping with work and a social or family life. A little planning and very little time, however, can make coupon use alone represent a major savings on grocery and household products.

Here's how I do it. First, reading the Sunday paper is a part of my "catching up with myself" routine, and that includes pulling all the coupon sheets. I spend a few minutes going through the coupons and cut out the ones for products I usually use or would like to try. I use scissors rather than try to tear them on the perforated lines, which is too frustrating!

A coupon box or folder is handy to keep coupons organ-ized. I know I would not be able to cope with them without one. I usually file my coupons at a later time on one of those evenings when I actually have time to watch the news. About once a month, I go through the coupons and throw away the ones that have expired.

Some people go through their coupons before going to the grocery store, remove the coupons they want to use, and attach them to their shopping lists. That's a good system for those who plan their trips to the grocery store in advance. Because I often teach early evening classes and have a schedule of other activities that changes often, I rarely know in advance when I will be able to get to the store, so I simply keep the coupon box in the car and keep my 4" x 6" card shopping list in my appointment book in my purse. Then when I am able to get to the store on the way home, I have everything I need. I keep a clip on the front of my coupon box, and as I put a coupon item in the basket, I clip the coupon to the front so that it is easy to give them to the checker.

I am not as organized in my coupon use as one friend, who calculates all her savings, shops double and triple coupons, and is able to accumulate many grocery and household items at no cost. She even accumulates items she does not use when she can combine sales and triple coupons so that she receives the items free. She then donates the items to various food drives for charitable groups. With the thirty minutes or so a week I spend on coupons, I am able to save 20% or more. She is able to save far more, but she is neither learning disabled nor employed outside the home. I think my investment of time pays off well, but more time spent would not get me enough additional savings to make it worthwhile.

Running Errands

You know how it is. You have to take a suit to the cleaners and pick up the things you took there last week, take shoes to be repaired, cash a check, and stop at the hardware store for nails, a caulking gun, and a tube of caulking. You go out and do your errands, and halfway through you realize that you took the suit to be cleaned, but forgot to pick up last week's cleaning. Or you have to backtrack because you didn't plan your stops in advance.

I use my 4" x 6" cards for errands, too. I write the stops in a reasonable order to cut down on my driving, and I list whatever I need to do at each stop. My list may look something like this:

Cleaners-
 take blue suit
 pick up tan dress
  grey jacket

Bank-cash check

Plaza Shoes-
 black flats – get heels
 brown shoes – half soles

Elliot's Hardware-
 finishing nails
 clear caulking (tube)
 caulking gun

Sometimes, I may just list the steps I have to make. That usually is enough for me. I also find that because I am a visual learner, just making the list may be enough to remind me of all my stops and what I need to do at each one. Since I work so far from home, and my schedule may not be the same every day because of teaching night classes or visiting the public schools, I usually have to schedule errands such as these during my hectic day. By making a list, I can usually get all of these sorts of things done while I am on my way to and from work.

Ordinary Reminders and the Use of Technology

Just as we can use technology to help us with academic tasks, we can use it to help us in other areas of our lives as well. For example, some learning disabled people I know use tiny pocket tape recorders for their lists. Instead of writing down something they need to remember, they just put it on tape. As a visual learner, I find notes more useful, but I do occasionally use a tape recorder.

Sometimes, when there is something I need to remember to do as soon as I get home, I call my home telephone number and leave myself a message on my telephone answering machine. My "getting home" routine always entails checking the machine for messages, so I'm sure to find the message from myself. I can then take care of it at once or write it down and post it where I am sure to see it later.

Posting notes to yourself or someone else may not be high technology, but it is a technique that can be extremely helpful. We have already discussed the use of a note board, either the chalkboard or whiteboard variety, on which grocery lists, telephone messages, or messages to others can be kept. Some families use an adaptation of this by leaving messages for one another on the telephone answering machine, especially if they have a machine that can retrieve messages from another location and then leave them on the machine for another family member to monitor later. Others use a home computer to leave messages or a tape recorder left in some agreed-upon spot in the house.

The use of notes of the written kind can be made more effective by taking care in deciding where to post them. For example, a note with a reminder to take out the trash is hard to miss if it is taped to the doorknob one must use to go out of the house! Notes for family members can be taped to the center of a bathroom mirror or some other hard-to-miss location.

Of course,sometimes you don't need to use notes as a reminder. That book you need to return to the library is hard to forget if you prop it against the door so that it falls on your foot when you open the door. You might do the same with the trash bag you need to remember to take out, so that you can't open the door without moving it. Just be careful you don't block the door and create a safety hazard is case of fire!

Getting Housework Done

Organization is something that troubles most of us LD people. Once we get organized, though, there's no limit to what we can do. Sometimes a schedule is helpful so that you get things done a little at a time rather than have them all pile up so that they are too much for you. I try to do a certain amount every day, but when my schedule of work, classes, out-of-town trips, and speaking engagements begins to stack up, and I am not able to take care of everyday tasks, I begin to get overwhelmed. Luckily, when the end of the semester comes, I can take some time to get all the things done that have accumulated. Unfortunately, this means I may not have as much time for fun and rest as I would like.

Organizing Tasks

One thing that can save a great deal of time is to figure out which things can be done together and which things cannot. Sometimes it would be very convenient if I could do a load of laundry, wash my hair, and run the dishwasher at the same time, but my water heater could never keep up, so that's out! I may have to schedule things a little differently to get it all done.

There are advantages to having a washer and dryer at home, but there are also advantages to taking your laundry to a laundromat to do it. Even though it is a lot of trouble to bundle it up, get all the supplies, and be sure you have enough change for the machines, you will be able to do it all at one time when you get there. I used to take paperwork to work on while the washers or dryers were running, so I would not be wasting time.

Some people organize their housecleaning by doing all of one room on one day, all of another on the next day, and so forth. That doesn't work for me because I would have to get out the vacuum cleaner and put it away too many times.

Other people do all the vacuuming on one day, the dusting on another, damp-mop the kitchen floor on another, scrub the bathrooms on another, and so forth. This may work well for you and may only take a few minutes each day.

My approach may not be good for you, but it is helpful for me. Because my schedule is so varied, I usually have only one day every week or every other week for general house cleaning. I may begin by putting things away that were left out on days when I was rushed, but I try to chain my movements so that finishing one task begins another. I may start by picking up a coat, sweater, and purse from a chair and hanging them in the closet. I'll take a stack of empty hangers and the dirty laundry from the hamper in the closet to the laundry room. That's where the vacuum cleaner is kept, so I'll bring it in, beginning my vacuuming from the nearest room, and so on.

A non-learning disabled friend watching me clean house with my system said it was the most disorganized thing she had ever seen, and it made her crazy! Maybe that's because she was trying to follow me around and talk to me while I was working, and I kept moving. The only important thing about my system is that it works – *for me*. You can try someone else's system and adjust it to your own needs or your own way of doing something. If your way works, there's no need to change. If you find a problem or something you're not getting done well, that's the time to try a new approach.

Job Lists

One approach some people find helpful is to list the jobs involved in cleaning, decide which ones to do on a particular day or weekend, and check them off as they are finished. I do this sometimes, especially if I am cleaning for a party, and I want to be sure I don't forget something. There is a very satisfying feeling in checking off the jobs as I get them done. Sometimes I start with one or two quick, easy jobs so that I can see my progress when I look at the list and have something to check off in a hurry. This helps when I am having trouble getting myself motivated to get things done.

Keeping Organized

I find that once things get disorganized, it takes forever to get them straight. Sometimes when I am very rushed, I forget that little things I don't take care of right away are going to pile up or get lost, and the scramble to take care of them will be much more damaging later on. Like many learning disabled people, I am able to make a big mess of things, and then it takes me forever to straighten them out.

A big problem for me, as it is for many of us, is losing things. If I don't put an important bill in a particular place, I may forget to pay it until it is overdue or be unable to find it later. In the stress of trying to find things in a hurry, I may look for something in the same place five or six times, be absolutely sure it is not there, and then find it in exactly that same place later.

It is a joke at my office that when I cannot find something, I call my secretary to help me. As soon as she walks in my office and begins to look, I will find it myself in one of the places I have already searched. The reason, of course, is that I am feeling less stressed when I know that she is there to help me.

To avoid these problems, I try to take just a few extra seconds to put things where they belong the first time I handle them although obviously I am not always perfect at following my own advice. One of the best rules of organization is to handle things as few times as necessary. For many things, this means only having to handle them once. For example, when you open the mail, drop the empty envelopes in the trash can at once, and only keep the letters or bills unless there is an address you need that appears only on the envelope (and this is usually true only of personal letters). This system is much more efficient than opening all the mail, then sorting it out later, and carrying the trash and letters or bills to two separate places.

A Place for Everything

Because my memory is so poor, I find that having a place for certain things and trying to keep them there works much better than trying to remember where I put things every time I use them. My purse, therefore, is always on the stepstool in the kitchen, and my keys are always in my purse. When I go out for my morning walk, I use a separate keyring with only the house key on it, and I always put it back in the same place.

Bills go in a basket as soon as I have opened them so that when I do my once-a-month bill paying, they are all ready to go. After I have read the paper, it goes in a stack to be bundled.

For things that I must remember to take to work, I have a canvas tote bag. If there's something that must come home from the office, I put it in the bag as soon as I think of it. That way, in the early-morning or late-afternoon rush, I don't have to try to think of everything I must take with me. Because my office is almost 40 miles from my home, running back home for something I have forgotten is impractical though I have had to do it on a few occasions!

To get really well organized, you might want to use a system developed by an expert in organization. I have recommended two excellent books, one on organization and one on eliminating clutter, in the Resource section at the end of this chapter.

Rewards

There's an old saying that work expands to fill up all the time you have to do it in. That can mean that if this is the weekend during which you planned to get things done, it may take the whole weekend. Did you ever notice that scheduling an activity you enjoy – a movie or a good friend coming over – can make you zip through your work in half the time it usually takes? If I have only an hour before a favorite TV program comes on, it's amazing how much I can get done!

Sometimes it is helpful to schedule a reward for yourself to keep yourself going. You can set your kitchen timer or alarm clock for a certain amount of time, plan to finish all of a particular task by the time the bell rings, and then take a break for something you enjoy. It can be as simple a reward as calling a friend for a chat, stopping for a walk or a soft drink, or listening to a little music.

It doesn't matter how minor the reward is. You'll still find you get much more work done in a shorter time than you would have if you had worked through the reward time!

Summary

Living with ourselves is something we all must do. Learning to work around our learning disabilities in keeping our home life organized and reasonably neat may be important in helping us to give ourselves a haven from our struggles to cope with the rest of the world. Using simple strategies to make household tasks easier can make a difference in keeping our home exactly that – a haven of peace and order.

Suggested Resources:

Aslett, Don. (1991). *Not for packrats only.* New York: Penguin.
This book is helpful in dealing with one of the big
organizational problems many of us have, which is keeping
too much stuff because we're not sure what is important and
what is not. Aslett helps you learn how to "de-junk" your
home and your life.

Hedrick, Lucy H. (1990). *Five days to an organized life.* New
York: Dell.
This step-by-step guide to organizing your life is ideal for
someone who would like to be better organized, but does not
know where to begin. Examples, charts, and lists are given in
a simple, straightforward style that is easy to read.

Chapter 8

Jobs: Getting Them and Keeping Them

A job. For many of us, the first job was the sign that we really were OK, that the learning disability was not going to mean that we were unable to be reasonably normal, capable, independent adults. For others, the first job was a disaster, as were maybe a few more. Sometimes even trying to get a job was a disaster when those LD characteristics popped up to hide our real abilities or led us to behave in some inappropriate way. Still others of us found ourselves in jobs far below our abilities or training because of problems other than those directly related to the job itself. If finding out about your learning disability is something new, you may finally be able to see why you had trouble getting a job, performing some work on the job, or keeping a job.

This chapter will discuss many job-related issues, from looking for a job and going to an interview to keeping a job. Because learning disabled adults with many different backgrounds are reading this book, you may have to skip around in this chapter to find the sections that apply to your situation. The headings will help you find what you want to know.

A good first step is to talk to a vocational counselor. If you are still in school and only thinking of dropping out, go to your school counselor before making that decision. There may be a number of work-study options that can be arranged for you. Your academic struggles may not seem so great when you are spending part of your day away from school involved in on-the-job training for a job you enjoy and are earning some money as well. Your counselor can tell you far more about what is available in your community than I can here, so start by asking him or her. Find out what programs are already going on in your school district that may be right for you.

Vocational Rehabilitation

Whether you are already out of school or thinking of dropping out, you should consider contacting your regional Vocational Rehabilitation office. Vocational Rehabilitation is a program with federal and state connections that can assist you as a learning disabled person to get appropriate training for employment. While you may have to pay for part of your training, depending on your income, in some cases your training may be completely covered.

To be eligible for Vocational Rehabilitation assistance, you will have to establish that you meet the criteria for learning disability, that your learning disability is a handicap affecting your employability, and that it can be expected that Vocational Rehabilitation can help you achieve employability. The training you receive can range from job training to college training for a profession, depending on your individual abilities and needs.

Because the services for which you may be eligible under Vocational Rehabilitation are varied and complex, you will need more information than is practical to give here. Look for Vocational Rehabilitation in the telephone directory or call information. You might also want to order information from HEATH Resource Center listed at the end of this chapter.

Types of Vocational Training

Many private vocational schools also provide training in many fields. Some schools specialize just in computer training. Others may provide office training as well. Electronics, automobile mechanics, and heavy equipment maintainance programs are provided by some vocational schools. Even long distance trucking can be learned through private training schools. A variety of programs in food service, including bartending, may be available. Private vocational schools provide training for many jobs in medical-related fields and in the fashion industry as well.

The schools vary widely in what they provide. Some offer job placement assistance after you complete their training. Some private vocational schools work with Vocational Rehabilitation, and their programs can sometimes be paid for if they are part of a job training program worked out for you by a rehabilitation counselor. You will want to check on all these possibilities.

One concern about vocational schools that has been in the news lately is whether or not they are reliable. While many are above reproach, a number of unscrupulous people have been involved in vocational training scams. The training has been inadequate or overpriced, and in some cases, the so-called trainers have disappeared almost overnight. In some particularly distressing cases, students had signed contracts with loan companies or banks rather than the schools themselves to pay for their training. Even though the school may have closed and the managers disappeared, the students still have had to make the payments on training they did not receive. The bottom line is to check thoroughly before signing any contracts. Check any schools you may be considering with the Better Business Bureau in your town as well as your Vocational Rehabilitation counselor. If you have a family lawyer, it is a good idea to have him or her look over any contracts before you sign them.

First Jobs

If you are a young adult with a learning disability, you may be looking for your first job. Whether you are looking for a part-time job of a type you wouldn't want to work at for the rest of your life or for a dream job that might be the beginnings of a real, lifelong career, this is an important experience for you. You will want to prepare well.

For example, even if the job you are applying for is as a bag boy at a supermarket or counter help at a fast food restaurant, there is some background work you can do that will help you in an interview. You can look in the telephone directory to see how many stores in the chain are located in your city. You can visit

129

one of the locations if you are not familiar with it already to look it over and familiarize yourself briefly with the way things are laid out.

Of course, you will want to be sure you have prepared a résumé. Yes, even for a first job, it is helpful to have a one-page résumé of your background. Include your name, address, and telephone number. For this type of job, adding your Social Security number might be a good idea. Give your educational background by indicating your high school and any additional education, such as college work or other training. Any jobs you have held, even part-time or volunteer work, should be indicated. You might list one or two references (with their permission), giving telephone numbers. All this should be neatly typed and carefully checked for proper spelling. You can run a few copies at your local copy center. Of course, you may still have to fill out a formal application form, but having all this information will make that task easier, and if a formal application form is not required, the employer will have something in hand that will enable him or her to reach you if you are the successful candidate for the job.

Calling About a Job

Let's say you've seen an ad in the newspaper or a sign in the window advertising for an employee. Your first step might be to call for an interview. Have paper and pencil handy, a calendar (or your appointment book if you keep one), and a copy of that résumé you prepared.

Look over the ad one more time. Is there a name of someone you need to speak to, or a title? Or is there just the telephone number? Make your call. Give your name and ask to speak to the person or title in the ad. If he or she is not in, ask when you might call back. If you get through to the person doing the hiring, restate your name and indicate you're calling about the job. From then on, you probably will find yourself answering questions. If an interview is wanted, by having your calendar handy, you can easily agree to a date and time that you can be available. Then you're on your way.

If all this makes you nervous, get a friend, parent, or someone else to practice with you. Practice a variety of possibilities so that you will be well prepared. Situations you might try include:

- –the person you need to speak to is not in, so you must find out when to call back;
- –the employer is there, but he says it's a busy time and you need to talk later;
- –the person who answers the telephone is the person doing the hiring.

The person helping you practice may think of other possibilities just to help you get used to the telephone situation.

Dressing for an Interview

Rules are changing about what clothing is appropriate for what occasion. Once I even saw a man in jeans, denim jacket, and run-down boots escorting a grandly dressed woman wearing jewels and a fur coat at the opera! Dressing for an interview is different, though. The impression you want to make is that you are perfectly "suited" for the job they have to fill, down to the last detail – and that may include your suit!

Even if the job you're applying for will require you to wear a uniform, how you dress for your interview makes an impression. You will need to be clean and neat, of course, but what you choose to wear is important as well. You will want to plan carefully what you will wear for your interview and be sure that everything you need is clean and in good repair. If you can afford only one interview outfit, keep it ready to go and don't wear it for other occasions.

As we will see in the next section, what you decide to wear may depend on the kind of job you are applying for or the place you hope to be working, so there are many things you will have to consider is selecting an interview outfit. You may have to have more than one kind of outfit if you are applying for several different types of jobs.

To be appropriately dressed for an interview, I believe that you need to be just a little better dressed than you think you would need to be on the job. If the job is in labor, and jeans will be worn on the job, it is generally still better to wear clean, washable pants that are *not* blue denim and a buttoned shirt or blouse rather than a T-shirt. Running shoes or tennis shoes are usually not appropriate, even though they are often more expensive than "hard" shoes or boots.

For most white-collar jobs, you probably should also dress just a little more conservatively than you think you might need to while actually on the job. This is the same advice I give my students who are training to become teachers. I tell them that when they are practicum students or student teachers working in the schools, they should go for their first visit very conservatively dressed, and after that just a little more conservatively dressed than the teachers in the school. This is important because prospective employers often judge applicants more strictly than they judge employees they have come to know or than they themselves!

I remember one student who did not take my advice. On her first visit to a school where she would be assisting a teacher who would be writing a recommendation for her, she wore a very attractive, well-tailored suit, but one that had knee-length, tailored shorts instead of a skirt. The outfit was fashionable and not extreme, but the classroom teacher, who often wore very casual, *very* short mini-skirts, T-shirts, and tennis shoes, graded her low on professional appearance and mentioned the shorts suit specifically as an inappropriate outfit for a teacher trainee!

The safest advice for women is: If you know that others at the job place wear suits, wear a suit for the interview. If others wear dresses, wear a suit or a dress with a jacket. If others wear slacks, wear a not-too-dressy dress or a skirt and blouse. Definitely wear hose! If others wear jeans, you might apply wearing a very tailored slacks outfit, but you are safer to wear a skirt and blouse. You don't want to be so much better dressed that you appear silly, but you need to be just a little more formal or conservative than you will need to be later if you get the job.

Dressing for an interview in food service may vary, depending on whether you are applying for a fast-food job or a job in an upscale restaurant. In either case, being scrupulously clean is essential. It's important for all job interviews, of course, but especially in food service. Whether you are a man or a woman, your hair will need to be clean, neat, and controlled. Don't make the interviewer have to imagine if you will be able to keep your waist-length, fly-away hair styled in a way that the Health Department will approve.

For office or sales work, men should wear suits and ties, and women should wear suits or coordinated outfits with jackets. If the sales job will be in a position selling clothing, the outfit should be comparable to the best-quality you can afford that is sold by that store. Here is where the exceptions come in: Whether you're male or female, if you are applying to work for a clothing store or other establishment that caters to more casual, modern, or even far-out customers, you will want to wear something a little more in keeping with the merchandise you hope to be selling. To apply for work in a cutting-edge young adult fashion store wearing a navy blue conservative suit might be too far from the norm for the interviewer to judge if you would fit in!

You might take a word of advice about two very touchy subjects, jewelry and perfumes. Perhaps more than any other area of dressing, people express themselves through accessories and scent. Because they are such personal expressions, however, there is always the risk that they may not be to the taste of the person in charge of hiring.

Jewelry should be simple and limited. For women, the less jewelry, the better. Dangling earrings should definitely not be worn for an interview. There's plenty of time later to wear favorite jewelry if it turns out to be acceptable in the particular job site.

For men, the old advice is still best: A watch and perhaps a wedding ring is the limit. Even though more and more men are wearing earrings, wearing one (or more) in a job interview may mean having the opportunity to express one's individuality while remaining unemployed.

It's usually best in dressing for an interview to avoid perfume or aftershave altogether. Most people have trouble judging how much is enough and how much is too much, and people with learning disabilities are no exception. Your interviewer may be allergic to certain fragrances or may simply not share your taste in fragrances. It is safer to eliminate the perfumes completely. If you're fresh and clean, and you've used soap, water, toothpaste, and deodorant, you should be as sweet-smelling as required.

Special Concerns

Most of the above information is what you might find in any book on dressing for an interview. What special guidelines should you keep in mind if you are learning disabled? It will be important for you to plan in advance how to keep any of those characteristics associated with learning disability from causing you problems with your clothing during an interview.

First, look over this list of the kinds of problems some learning disabled people have related to clothing or grooming. Check those which apply to you:

Men or women:

_____Trouble keeping shirt or blouse tucked in

_____Don't notice food spots on clothing

_____Uncomfortable or uneasy in new clothing

_____Trouble matching colors

_____Poor sense of style or fit

_____Difficulty selecting appropriate style for occasion

_____Poor skills at ironing, pressing, or mending clothing

_____Forgetting to check appearance for details

Women:

_____Awkwardness in some shoes, such as high heels or shoes
with slippery soles

_____Trouble sitting gracefully in short skirts

_____Difficulty in managing purse and briefcase or other hand-
carried items when handshaking, etc.

_____Unawareness of uneven or worn-off makeup or untidy,
wind-blown hair

_____Awkwardness with hand-carried items, such as purses

If you are not sure if you have any of the above problems,
make a point of asking someone you trust to describe honestly
those areas with which you need help. Then plan accordingly. The
best way to deal with these problems is to try to avoid them if you
can. For example, the obvious way to avoid awkwardness caused
by high-heeled shoes is to plan to wear attractive shoes with a
more comfortable heel height. Often, the best solution is simple.

Here are some possible solutions to the problems above:

Shirttail problems: For men, be sure your shirt is long enough to
tuck in well. Then adjust your belt tightly enough to keep it snug
either sitting or standing. Not too tight – you don't want to spend

the entire interview in misery!

For women, one problem is that many women's skirts have a waistband without belt loops. When women's waist measurements vary by an inch or more – as most women's waist measurements do during their monthly cycles – a fit that is either too tight or too loose can cause problems. If possible, avoid skirts without beltloops. If you tend to be one of us who gets dressed in the morning and forgets to check clothing adjustments in the mirror during the day, you might consider selecting an interview dress that has few such problems. For example, a very professional look can be achieved with a jacket dress. Often, these look like suit-and-blouse combinations, but because the dress under the jacket is sewn together at the waist seam and covered with a belt, there is no shirttail to creep out.

For interview situations where a less formal look is appropriate, choose a one-piece dress rather than a skirt and blouse look. If a two-piece look is desired, a soft cotton knit blouse or shirt (but not a collarless T-shirt) gives a good appearance and tends to stay put better than one made of woven fabric.

Spots or missing buttons: If you are often surprised when someone points out you've spilled coffee on your clothes or you discover a big spill, ripped seam or missing button when you get home and wonder if it's been that way all day, you will want to be sure you don't make a poor appearance at an interview. Make a point of checking over the outfit you plan to wear the night before an interview. Check again in the restroom mirror at the location of the interview ahead of time. With outfits that are worn more than once before laundering or drycleaning, check it over again when you take it off. Then hang it carefully to avoid wrinkles.

Uneasy in new clothing: Don't wear something brand-new for an interview. If you need a new outfit for an interview, wear it for at least a couple of hours a day or so before your interview. See how it behaves when you sit and stand two or three times. If it is uncomfortable, bunches up somewhere or gaps somewhere else, or has to be tugged into place often, you will be uncomfortable throughout your interview, and it may affect how you behave. You would do better to select another outfit.

Once you have given an interview outfit a trial run, check it over to see if it needs pressing or cleaning. Then hang it carefully so that it will be ready for your interview.

Trouble matching colors or patterns: Have a friend or relative who always looks well-put-together help you select a complete outfit that goes together. Be sure to check everything you will be wearing, including shoes, socks or stockings, and accessories. Your advisor can also let you know if a hem needs shortening or lengthening or if there are other details that need work or some part of your outfit, such as a belt, that might need replacing.

Poor sense of style or fit; difficulty in selecting appropriate style for occasion: Have your trusted friend who has a good sense of style go with you when you buy clothing. You will have to define you budget limitations, of course, but a person with a good eye for clothing can help you get the most for your money in terms of something that looks good on you. Some of us just don't have good judgment on clothing and can buy even very expensive clothing and look shabbily dressed. There are fashion counselors who can be hired to go through everything in a person's wardrobe, showing what should be kept and what should be thrown away, and then advise on what should be purchased. It's an expensive service, but perhaps your friend can go through your closet with you and help you select outfits that go together well. He or she can also advise you on what to wear for which occasion. You might want to make a list to keep inside your closet door of some appropriate outfits.

Poor skills at ironing, pressing, or mending clothing: If you hate to iron or don't iron well, it will be very important for you to shop carefully and avoid clothing that will need special care. Of course, if you can afford to have everything done at the laundry or dry cleaners, that will not be a problem, but not everyone wants to spend the money. The current trend to natural fibers like cotton means a return to ironing. If you don't like to iron or to pay for cleaning, don't buy things that need it.

Synthetics and blends are easier to care for, but they take some attention. If you remove items from the dryer promptly and put them on hangers, they usually take little or no ironing unless they are all cotton or linen. This means you have to remember to take them out as soon as the dryer stops tumbling – and remembering to pay attention to such things is not a strong ability for most people with learning disabilities. I often take a small kitchen timer with me when I work on some other project while the dryer is running. When it rings, I am almost always startled and find I have forgotten all about the dryer. The timer makes it possible for me to get things on hangers before they get wrinkled and need ironing. Mending is another matter. Because many people with learning disabilities tend to be a bit clumsy, we often have ripped hems or torn linings in our clothing. I have skirts I have had to fix repeatedly, all caught on the same car door! If you are not skilled at sewing and mending, you may want to barter with someone who is or locate a professional service to do the work for you. Sometimes a dry cleaning establishment will provide inexpensive repairs to clothing that they will also be cleaning. It may be worth an occasional cleaning bill to get inexpensive repairs done as well.

Forgetting to check appearance for details: It is essential that your last stop before an interview be somewhere you can go over your appearance one last time. Is your clothing tidy, your hair neat? One of my own appearance problems is in this area. I fix my hair and put on my make-up in the morning, and it is sometimes late afternoon when I realize I haven't looked in a mirror all day. I look and discover that I am both pale and tousled! I have at least trained myself to do a last-minute check before I make a speech.

138

Awkwardness with hand-carried items, such as purses: There are two good ways to deal with purse problems in an interview session. One, perhaps the obvious one, is not to carry one. If you are wearing a suit or dress with a jacket, your driver's license and car keys (*not* a whole rattling ring of keys) and a tissue might be slipped into a pocket.

I find I feel insecure without my purse, so a second option seems better for me: Using a small purse with a shoulder strap. I normally carry a very large shoulder bag, but for circumstances such as an interview, a smaller bag is preferable. It can be large enough to contain make-up for a possible touch up in the ladies' room before the interview as well as other papers that might be needed. Just be sure that the purse is neat, and things you might need are easily accessible without digging.

Many women are now opting not to carry purses at all just at a time when purses for men are becoming acceptable. Some carry what they might need in a purse in a briefcase and thus only have one hand-carried item to deal with. For many job situations, however, a briefcase is not appropriate. Take a little time to determine what will work best for you.

The Interview

The interview is often a make-or-break situation for a learning disabled applicant. No matter how good the training, the letter of application, or the recommendations, that face-to-face meeting with the prospective boss is extremely important. The most important trick here is to be prepared.

First, know as much as possible about the employing firm. Even if it is a fast-food establishment, you can find out at least a little about it ahead of time. If you have not eaten there, go to one of their locations. Look over the menu to become familiar with the prices and the type of food. Look in the telephone directory to see how many locations they have in town. With larger firms, you can call or visit the public library and ask the librarian to help you find out a little about the firm. In some cities, the Chamber of Commerce will have flyers or other information about large corporations in town. If you are applying to work for one of them, this can be very helpful. You might also call the public relations office of a firm and ask for information.

A second way to be prepared for an interview is to practice being interviewed. Get a friend or family member to help you out, playing the role of the prospective boss. Practice coming into the office, shaking hands (women may suddenly realize that it is important to carry the purse in the left hand or on the left shoulder in order to shake hands easily).

What sorts of questions should you be prepared to answer? You will want to be able to say where you have worked in the past and for how long, without having to pause for a long time to remember dates or places. You will want to be prepared to respond when asked why you are no longer employed at a certain place. If you were fired or if you quit under pressure, you might want to practice discussing the situation and indicate that you have learned from the experience.

Perhaps the most difficult part of an interview for many people is discussing salary or wages. You will definitely want to practice this. In some cases, there is little room for discussion. In most cases, however, it is recommended that you, as the person being interviewed, not bring up the subject. Further, if you are asked what salary or wages you expect to be paid, you probably should simply say that you would expect to be paid in accordance with your experience, but that you would hope your work would make you eligible for appropriate raises in the future.

Mentioning your learning disability is certainly something you will want to consider. If you will be applying for a job that will not be affected by your learning disability, then it is not something you need to bring up. If, however, you think it may be a problem and you may need some accommodation on the job, you will want to practice talking about it.

Because the Americans with Disabilities Act ensures that employers must make reasonable accommodations for workers with disabilities, including learning disabilities, this should not be a problem, but you do not want to be abrasive or demanding. Your practice partner can help you work on logical, appropriate ways to discuss your specific type of learning disability and the accommodations that might be appropriate.

Another important part of the interview to practice is knowing when it is at an end. An interview may last anywhere from 15 minutes to an hour, usually depending on the type of job – the higher paid the job, the longer the interview is likely to be. The following are some signals that time is up that you will want to practice observing and responding to:

Spoken signals that the interview is ending:

"Well, thank you for coming in. We'll be in touch."

"We'll call you in a day or so with our decision."

"Mr. Johnson, your next interview is waiting."

"Now, do you have any questions about the job?" (If so, be sure to ask. If not, say more than just *"No."* Try *"No, thanks, I think you have explained everything. I appreciate the chance to interview for the job."*

Other signals that mean the interview is ending:

The interviewer stands up and offers his or her hand.

The interviewer places your application in a file and closes it.

The interviewer walks you to the office or store door.

When one of these signals occurs, you might extend you hand, thank the interviewer for seeing you and leave. If there is a secretary or receptionist, be sure to say goodbye to him or her as well.

If the interview is likely to be in a less formal setting than an office, such as in a restaurant or outdoor setting, practice in that type of setting also.

Arriving for the Interview

Allow more than enough time to arrive for your interview. One man with learning disabilities always goes to the location a day or two before the scheduled interview just to be certain he knows how to get there. He allows extra time because he can't be sure what traffic will be like at a different time of day. While you don't want to arrive in the office an hour ahead of time, you *can* arrive outside the building early and wait to enter the office until about ten minutes ahead of your scheduled time.

Be sure to make a stop at the rest room before your interview. Check to make sure your clothing is neat and in order and that your hair is tidy and your hands clean. Women will want to check their make-up. Again, this is *not* the time to add perfume.

Interview Behavior

If your interview is in an office or store setting, there will probably be a receptionist or secretary who will greet you. Give your name and what you're there for, perhaps something like this:

"Hello. I'm Janet Smith, and I'm here for an 11:00 appointment with Mr. Johnson."

The secretary or receptionist will probably have you sit in the reception area until time for your appointment. You will need to sit quietly and wait. If the secretary is typing or working, don't interrupt with casual talk or questions. If you feel you will be nervous just sitting quietly, it's acceptable to pick up a magazine to look at, but be prepared to get up as soon as you're called for your appointment. Have your application and résumé ready. If you're offered a cup of coffee, decline it with thanks unless you are much more adept with such situations than most of us with learning disabilities. You don't want to risk a spill or awkwardly having to deal with the coffee if you are called for your appointment before you have finished.

Be sure that your right hand is free because in most interview situations you will be expected to shake hands. Don't carry anything in your right hand because you will have to make an awkward transfer before you can offer your hand.

As you enter the office, watch for a signal about where you are to sit if there are several chairs. If you are not sure, ask simply, "Where would you like me to sit?" If you are seated near the interviewer's desk, don't put anything on the surface of the desk. Keep your papers (and for a women, your purse) either in your lap or within reach on the floor.

Answering Questions

Since you've practiced for your interview, you know you are ready for most questions. If one is asked for which you are not prepared, it's acceptable to think about it, or to say you might need more information.

Filling Out Applications

The application form is often a major problems for a prospective worker who has learning disabilities. Putting down information in writing in small blanks on a long form can be a nightmare. If at all possible, obtain a copy of the blank form ahead of time and indicate that you will bring or send it back. Then you can take it home and fill it in carefully. If you have only one copy of the form, and this is usually the case, stop at a copy center and make two or three photocopies. Then you can fill in one completely in pencil for practice before transferring your answers to the good form or before having someone do it for you.

If you fill out the form yourself, be sure to have someone look it over for omissions or errors.

It is important to be accurate and honest in filling out application forms. If there is a question about your learning disability, it will probably ask if you have a disability that will affect your work. Remember that covering up your disability won't work if you can't do the job once you have been hired. The law states that if you are able to do the work with reasonable accommodation, you can't be discriminated against, so give the information that is needed as it relates to your job capability.

Employment Testing

Sometimes a written test is required as part of a job application procedure. If taking written tests is a problem for you, you will need to let the employer know whether or not you can take the test. If additional time or other test accommodation can make a difference, you should request it. If the test itself is not related to the job you would be doing, you may be able to ask to have it omitted and an interview substituted.

Letters of Application

If a job requires a formal letter of application, it is important to produce a letter that will represent you well. After all, it is your introduction to the prospective employer. It is fascinating to hear employers describe the quality of letter of application they have received and how those letters often cause the rest of the application to be dropped into the wastebasket unread. Employers tell of misspelled, penciled letters written on lined notebook paper from applicants for professional or technical jobs requiring college degrees!

You will also want to include a copy of your résumé. If this is a beginning-level job, your résumé may be the simple one-page type that was described above. For most jobs, short résumés are generally preferred. If you have more than a little experience, you may want to look at a job guide for help in preparing a résumé suitable for your particular field. It seems that only in college teaching are long résumés acceptable, even desirable. I thought that mine was too long at seven pages until I served on a search committee and read some that were twenty and thirty pages long.

Letters of Reference

Frequently you will simple be asked to provide the names, addresses, and telephone numbers of two or three references. If so, be sure you have the permission of the people you have chosen to list and the addresses and telephone numbers they prefer that you use. Be sure to spell their names correctly and include the proper titles. Job-related references are usually best for a job application. If you have none of those, include teachers or others who can speak about your ability and work habits.

If letters of reference are requested, you will need to ask the required number of people to write references for you. Be prepared with a description of the job for which you are applying and the type of information needed for the reference. Contact your references and ask if they will be willing to recommend you. If you are talking to your references in person, you can give them a copy of:

- the job description;
- the name, title, and address of the person to whom the letter should go;
- a copy of your résumé to help refresh the reference's memory about your abilities;
- information as to when the reference needs to be received.

Keeping Your Job

Probably more of us lose our jobs for social and behavioral reasons than for lack of ability to do the work. Issues such as reliability (especially showing up on time), following through on instructions, and working well with others are areas in which people with learning disabilities need to be especially careful.

Time Problems: One office manager recently told me of an employee she had to fire because of constant tardiness. The employee had been warned repeatedly but continued to come in ten to fifteen minutes late in an office where the early morning workload was especially heavy. When given his last warning, the young man insisted he simple couldn't get to work on time. The manager suggested leaving home earlier. "I leave home in plenty of time," the employee replied, "but there's so much traffic it takes longer than I expect!" He simply didn't understand that his answer made no sense.

In most jobs, no matter how good your work is when you are there, the boss is justified in being upset if you are not there when you are supposed to be. It is your responsibility to be there on time, no matter how early you must leave home to get there and to return on time from breaks and from lunch. Employers often complain that the employees who are late to work are the ones most likely to be exactly on time to leave for break or at the end of the day. Make sure that you give the employer his or her full day's work, and you will already have gained many points as a reliable employee.

Following Instructions: Perhaps the problem is not so much in following instructions exactly but often in remembering what the instructions were. Making a list or even just a note or two to remind you what you need to accomplish can be extremely helpful. If you are given instructions you don't fully understand, it's usually better to ask for clarification at the time. If you find your supervisor becoming impatient or angry at your requests for more explanation, you may need to ask later for a conference in which you explain that you really want to do the job right, but that you may need repeated or clearer instructions from time to time. If you emphasize your desire to do good, error-free work, you should be able to get the help you need.

Social problems: One of the primary social problems that learning disabled people may have on the job is knowing when to socialize, when not to, and when stop. Much of the problem may have to do with interpreting things literally. For many of us, "Hi, how are you?" sounds like an invitation to tell all our physical troubles, rather than a simple greeting, the answer to which should be, "Fine, thanks, how are you?" We may end up standing at someone else's work station or desk continuing a conversation long past the time we should.

Another problem may be not noticing cues that indicate we have gone too far in some way. Just as we often have to practice knowing when an interview is over by watching carefully for certain signs that non-learning disabled people notice automatically, we sometimes need help in knowing when to drop a subject or leave the boss's office or just get back to work.

Special Issues: Your Rights Under the Law

If you received services under special education while you were still in school, you probably know that your rights to those services were guaranteed by Public Law 94-142 and others that preceded and followed it. Your rights as an adult with learning disabilities in the workplace and in public accommodation are guaranteed by other laws about which you should be aware. We will look at them briefly here, but you may wish to obtain more information about them by ordering the booklets listed in the Resources section at the end of this chapter.

Section 504: This is actually a section of the Rehabilitation Act of

1973, or Public Law 93-112. The law states that you have rights to employment and a variety of other services, just as non-disabled people do, from any public or private agency that receives federal financial assistance.

Your rights on the job include being considered for your ability, not your disability. Your employer must not discriminate against you because of your disability in hiring, promotion, layoffs, or any other job-related decisions. If you are not sure about these rights, your nearest Office for Civil Rights can advise you.

Americans with Disabilities Act: This act is an important extension of protection against discrimination in work, public service, transportation, and other areas. A major provision of the law is that an employer, for example, must make reasonable accommodations so that a qualified individual with a disability may perform work. This may include making a modification in the workplace or in certain aspects of the job that do not affect performance or results. Again, the Office for Civil Rights can help if you are not sure whether your job situation might be covered.

Summary

In today's world, much of adult status is determined by the ability to work. Doing worthwhile work in a job one enjoys and can do well is an important part of feeling fulfilled as a contributing member of society. Many people with learning disabilities have in the past had to work at jobs below their ability or aspirations or have had to find ways to hide their disabilities to find and keep jobs.

New laws, new training, and new sensitivity have made it possible for people with learning disabilities to have more opportunities than ever before. Whether your dream job is working with your hands or with your mind, its good to know that your prospects are outstanding.

Suggested Resources

Brown, Dale. (1982). *Rehabilitating the learning disabled adult.*
Washington, DC: President's Committee on Employment of
People with Disabilities.

Although this booklet is intended for rehabilitation
counselors, Dale Brown's personal writing style makes this
booklet readable and inspiring for learning disabled adults as
well. It includes case studies and an excellent section on types
of learning disabilities and how they may affect an employee
in a job situation.

Learning Disabilities Association of Canada. (1990). *Job
Interview Tips for People with Learning Disabilities.*

This excellent program includes both a book and an
audiocassette to help prepare you for a job interview and
more. It includes information on preparing résumés and a
variety of letters associated with finding a job. It can be
ordered either from the Canadian LDA, at 323 Chapel Street,
Suite 200, Ottawa, Ontario K1N 7Z2, or through the
American LDA at 4156 Library Road, Pittsburgh PA 15234.
Write for price information.

Other excellent resources available from HEATH Resource
Center (address can be found in the Resources section, p.226)
include:

1. *Young Adults with Learning Disabilities and Other Special
   Needs: Guide for Selecting Postsecondary Transition
   Programs.*

Included are checklists on readiness for the transition to the world of work, a list of transition centers, and selected publications, as well as a discussion of assistance for learning disabled young adults who need some support in entering the job market.

2. *Vocational Rehabilitation Services: A Postsecondary Student Consumer's Guide.*

This is a brief overview of Vocational Rehabilitation services in a question-and-answer format, and includes information on available services and eligibility for them.

Resources on Your Legal Rights

U.S. Department of Justice. (undated). *The Americans with Disabilities Act: Questions and Answers.*

This bulletin is available in a variety of formats, including computer disk and electronic bulletin board. In question-and-answer format, it covers the provisions of the act for employment, public accommodations, and miscellaneous provisions. Resources and contact agencies for specific requirements are included. The bulletin is available from:

Office on the Americans with Disabilities Act
Civil Rights Division
U,S, Department of Justice
P.O. Box 66118
Washington, DC 20035-6118

Department of Health and Human Services. (undated). *Your Rights as a Disabled Person.*

An especially useful feature of this bulletin is the listing of regional addresses and telephone numbers for the Office for Civil Rights. The bulletin details rights under Section 504 of the Rehabilitation Act of 1973. It is available from:

Department of Health and Human Services
Office for Civil Rights
Washington, DC 20202

Chapter 9

Staying Home or Coming Back: Living with Your Parents as an Adult with Learning Disabilities

It's been said that you can never really go home again once you're grown and gone. That's true to a certain extent. What it really means is that home is not the same when you return to live in your parents' home as an adult or when you continue to live at home at an age when most adults have established homes of their own. Yet this is a living arrangement some young adults with learning disabilities may find most workable, at least for a time. Financial problems, the economics of the country, marriage problems, or job problems may make it necessary for a young adult either to continue to live at home or to return to live with his or her parents temporarily.

We'll first look at the problems of the adult who returns home to live after being gone. Later, we'll examine some of the special problems that may be faced by young adults who are remaining in their parents' home as they work toward becoming independent and on their own for the first time.

Coming Home

Whatever problem may lead the adult with learning disabilities to return to the family home, what is important to remember is that there have been changes on all sides. As a young adult you have been seeking independence. Having found it to some degree, you can never return to the site of former dependence with quite the same attitude. Your parents, meanwhile, have gone through changes as well. Before you children were born, they were alone together and free to make their own schedules. With the arrival of the first child, all that changed, and their options and privacy became more limited. Then, as you and your brothers or sisters left home, your parents regained their privacy and independence. In some cases, the "empty nest" brought distress to parents who may have lived to a large extent for and through their children. In other cases, the empty nest was made even emptier by divorce or the death of a spouse.

With your return home, the family situation is changed once again. Examination of the implications of these changes can help you and your family avoid some problems and make your new family structure – more than just tolerable, but rather a positive, productive option for everyone.

Perhaps one of the most important factors to stress is that your return home as an adult must be seen as a result of a particular situation, whether it is the economy of the area of the country or a family situation, but not necessarily as a direct result of your learning disabilities. Neither you nor your parents should view the situation as a failure on the part of either, but as a temporary situation faced these days by many non-learning disabled families as well.

What is the impact of this alteration of the family on the adult with learning disabilities, on the parents, and on the family as a whole?

Impact on the Adult with Learning Disabilities

Let's look first at the effect of this return to the family home on you as an adult:

1. The return home may seem to you to be a symbol of a loss of independence. It may be difficult for you to overcome the impulse to see every situation at home as a test of your independence or your ability to be your own boss. Your parent's

simple question, "When will you be home this evening?" may seem to be prying when it may really be no more than a simple request for information needed to plan dinner. Try to keep a balanced perspective on such situations and don't be too quick to assume the worst. You can help by making sure that when your schedule affects others' schedules, you let people know what time to expect you.

2. Living at home, whether in the old room you lived in as child and teenager or in a newly-refurbished garage apartment, does entail a certain loss of privacy. Remember to respect others as you expect the same treatment. If you don't want a parent or sibling to come into your room without knocking, follow the same rules yourself. The hours you keep will be obvious to everyone. Whether you do your laundry regularly will be apparent and so will a dent in the fender. Whoever picks up the mail will see a late payment notice for the car, too. All of these are part of living in the same living space with others.

3. A mixed blessing is that in some cases you will have fewer opportunities to make your own mistakes. Of course, there may be the opportunity to make other mistakes, such as overestimating how far a paycheck will go when there is no apartment rent to pay.

4. Your friends, your music, your clothing, and your habits will obviously be under closer scrutiny than when you lived on your own. Tastes and choices that are new since you left home may startle family members who are used to the old you. You can expect some comments, possibly not all positive.

Suggestions

How can you as an adult deal with this impact on your life? Here are some suggestions:

1. First, remember that when you were living at home as a child, you had many rights and few responsibilities. As an adult, a responsibility comes with every right. For young adults returning

home, this is sometimes difficult to cope with.

If you feel you have the right not to be nagged, remember that you also have the responsibility to do those things you may have agreed to do. If you don't do them, you shouldn't be surprised when you are reminded!

2. Remember that your parents' lifestyle has also changed since you left home. You expect them to accept the fact that you've matured and changed; you must accept that they have changed, too. Your mother may have been a traditional stay-at-home mom and the world's best "from scratch" cook. While you were on your own, she may have discovered that frozen dinners prepared in the microwave aren't too bad and using them leaves her more time for jogging or ceramics, or she may have gone back to college or entered the job market.

3. Ask for help *before* it's a life-or-death situation. Certainly you want to make your own decisions, but help is much easier to get when there's more than one option open. Compare these situations:

"Dad, I'm concerned. I need to go to the dentist, but if I pay cash I don't see how I can make my car payment. Can you help me figure out what I want to do?"

or

"Hello, Dad? They've repossessed my car! I couldn't make the payment because I had to pay the dentist. Can you come pick me up? I know it's 3 A.M., but . . ."

4. Communicate! When you give information, you may solve many problems before they arise.

"Mom, that construction job on the east side may run late tonight, and there's no convenient place to call. I may miss supper."

"Don't worry if I'm not in 'til late. The concert will run really late, and a bunch of us will probably go out for breakfast after

it is over."

You may think Mom shouldn't be aware of when you come and go, but after years of listening for your footsteps before she could sleep peacefully, and then months or years of *not* having that responsibility, it may be hard for her to rest easily until she mentally tucks everyone in.

5. Watch your finances! Perhaps you came home for the same reason that many young adults have done so: Today's financial crunch made it impossible for you to go it alone right now. Whether you're paying your share of the family expenses or not, don't let the fact that you have more disposable income than before cause you to overextend yourself or you'll compromise your ability to work your way out on your own again.

No matter how much or how little you're making, you might try keeping two budgets: One that is practical for your present situation and one that shows what it would cost you to be living on your own. Looking over that second budget often will keep you from spending in ways that will prevent you from reaching your goal of being independent again.

6. Be considerate in your habits. You may have become used to playing your music loudly in the car with windows down, but driving up the driveway late at night with a heavy bass beat echoing up to your parents' bedroom window is neither considerate nor smart. Likewise, night-owl TV watching, which many adults with ADD enjoy, could be a problem if others in your house need to be up early.

Impact on Parents

What is the impact on the parent or parents of the adult's return home? Much depends on the overall family situation at the time as well as on the reasons for your return. Looking at possible problems your parents may face in advance and working with them to develop strategies to deal with these problems may help you and your parents avoid some pitfalls and will make the ones you do have easier to deal with.

Here are some of the specific problems your parents may face on your return home:

1. An immediate and sometimes unconsidered impact on your parents may be the loss of the privacy they have become used to again. Lazy weekend mornings and their own choice of TV or music may suddenly seem to be coming to an end. When the key turns in the door, your parents may be struck by the fact that it may not be just you catching them in old sweat pants and paint-splattered T-shirt – you may have brought a guest with you. When you were nine and brought a buddy home unexpectedly, your parents usually weren't embarrassed. Now your friends are other adults, and the situation is changed. Of course, if you still have younger brothers or sisters at home, this won't be as much of a problem, but a problem your parents will face instead is the following:

2. If there are still other children at home, a big set of problems may revolve around differences in the way you as a returning adult child expect to be treated and the way your brothers or sisters still at home are treated. Different expectations, in terms of both rights and responsibilities, may be appropriate, and it's a good idea to work them out carefully from the beginning. If you have other siblings who do not live at home, they may be concerned that you are taking advantage of your parents by moving back home or limiting their access to Mom and Dad as babysitters for the grandchildren.

3. Your parents' schedule may be less flexible unless you are eating no meals at home and living completely independently although within the same house or perhaps in the garage apartment. Your parents may have become used to changing meal plans or laundry day on a whim and now having your needs to consider may alter that.

4. There will certainly be some economic impact. This can be positive but is frequently negative, often more so than you might think. Your parents may insist on your not paying any part of the bills but may be shocked to find that your twice-a-day shower and

158

shampoo routine and your refrigerator raiding, not to mention your long-distance telephone calls, run up the bills more than they had thought possible. In other cases, shared living arrangements, with the returning adult sharing expenses as well, have been helpful to parents whose reduced income (through retirement, divorce, or death of a spouse) has caused lowered family income.

5. Another problem your parents will face depends on what the relationship was between you and them when you lived at home before. If you were identified as a handicapped child in previous years, you may have been overprotected to a certain extent. It's a natural response when worried parents must deal with something new and frightening, and it often takes time for them to overcome the impulse to "pad the corners" of the world to make life easier for a handicapped child. If that was the case for you, it probably took a long time for you and your parents to work out this situation. Your return home may bring out that impulse again, and both you and your parents may need help in dealing with it.

Suggestions for Parents

To help avoid possible problems, here are some suggestions that I have written in the form of advice directly to your parents. You may want to sit down and go over these ideas with them or just pass the book along for them to read for discussion later.

1. Don't nag. This is the hardest guideline to follow, but one of the most important for parents of adult children, with or without learning disabilities. Often we, as parents, regard as "helpful reminders" those very comments our children see as sheer, unadultered nagging. This was extremely difficult for me personally, as my daughter can attest. I think she matured to this problem before I did. Long before I was able to stop giving advice she hadn't asked for, she was able to smile and listen without angry retorts. Of course, she went ahead and made her own decisions!

2. Deal with problems by trying to head them off. Discussing an area of concern before a crisis occurs can often help. Waiting until some evening and asking, "Dennis, I've noticed that you had to skip breakfast all this week to get to work on time. Do you want me to stop fixing your breakfast, get you a new alarm clock, offer to wake you, or just hush up about it?" may be a better approach than seething as you feed cold scrambled eggs to the dog and eventually blow up.

3. Remember that you're no longer responsible for your son or daughter's taste in clothing, music, or friends. While you certainly reserve the right to set the rules for your home, try to consider them in the same light as you would had you rented the room or garage apartment to a stranger. Yes, you should be able to have absolute rules concerning such issues as drugs or alcohol, and you should be able to set rules concerning how loudly music may be played in your adult child's room. but rules about *which* music may be played? No.

4. Don't nag.

5. Work hard on respecting your adult child's privacy. Whether he or she is living in the same room as before leaving home or in a garage apartment on the property, consider how you would respect the privacy of an adult boarder in your home. You'd knock before entering; you wouldn't open mail or ask questions about the mail; you'd deliver telephone messages without a lecture. Learning to treat your adult child more as an adult than as your child may be difficult at first. When my daughter returned home for a time, she lived in the guest cottage behind my house. A rule we somehow adopted was that neither of us just dropped in on the other without telephoning even though we lived twenty-five feet apart! Friends (mine *and* hers) found it odd, but for both of us, it was a symbol that she was an adult, not a child.

6. Be sure that *all* family members know about the new arrangements. In some families, even those adult children not living at home will need to be informed of the arrangement, especially when it means the room upstairs is no longer available for weekend babysitting space for grandchildren. Younger

children still living at home should know, too, how the older sibling's return will affect their lives and plans. Problems will be decreased if they are in on the planning early on.

7. Be sure you've stated the non-negotiable issues clearly. If no smoking or drugs in the house is the rule, state it clearly, and state the consequences for infractions. Don't snoop, but if an infraction occurs, follow up as stated. Perhaps you're making the car payments by check, and the adult child is paying you in cash from each paycheck. Set in advance a cut-off date when, if payment is not forthcoming, the finance company will be called to pick up the car or the keys will be hung up. Again, which items are negotiable and which are not will vary from family to family.

8. See numbers 1 and 4 above.

9. Work out in advance what the financial arrangements will be. If your adult child is returning home because of financial problems related to poor money management, you will probably want and need to help set up a budget. It will be important that you do not simply take on all of his or her expenses. To do so will make it very difficult for the adult to regain independence. If an expensive car and many credit card bills are the problem, it may be important to arrange a budget to pay them off, but if the unwise spending continues while no room and board are being paid, you may be providing the kind of help that is smothering in the long run.

And if There Are Problems?

The impact of the adult's return home must be considered on the family as a whole and will depend on many factors. Changes in economic or emotional circumstances may make a difference. Not to be overlooked is the possibility that all may *not* go well. Unresolved difficulties from the past, or even new problems, may result in conflict. If a round-table, heart-to-heart discussion does not resolve the problems, then rather than dissolve the arrangement in despair, family counseling might be sought.

Private counseling, public agency counseling, or religious-affiliated counseling are all good possibilities, depending on your particular family circumstances.

Take a look at some of the type of counseling described in Chapter 5. Most of the helping professionals described their work with families as well as with individuals. Frequently, families find that counseling not only helps resolve the specific set of problems that brought them to seek help but also helps open new channels of communication and warmth.

The Young Adult Who Remains at Home

For the young adult with learning disabilities who remains at home, some of the circumstances may be different than for the adult who returns to the family home. For many, remaining at home is an option because a community college or job training in the home community is accessible and less expensive than going out of town. This is true for many non-learning disabled young adults as well. Many of us with learning disabilities, though, tend to be less mature than others at our age. For those of us with this problem, staying at home gives us just a little more time to mature into independent adults.

That movement to maturity is not a steady pace. One family, with a single-parent home, has two learning disabled sons, one of whom is still in high school and one who is in community college. The college-age son was not ready to leave home for an out-of-town college when he graduated from high school, but after working part-time and attending community college for two or three years, he is becoming confident of this maturity and readiness to be on his own. Though the younger brother often points to his brother's lapses, their mother wisely points out that her older son's maturity in judgment and behavior has steadily improved, and in spite of the setbacks along the way, the trend has always been upward.

The opportunity to make independent mature decisions may

not come easily to you if you are a young adult who has not been away from home. Your parents have been used to making decisions for you and to worrying about you, in part because of your learning disability. It may be hard for them to let go and give you a chance to make your own way, and, yes, to make some mistakes while you are learning.

You may find it helpful to work out some guidelines with your parents and set a timeline for when you will reach a certain level of independence even while you live at home. For example, you and your parents may agree that as soon as you have a part-time job or are enrolled in college or a job-training program, you will be on your own. (Meanwhile you may also decide, perhaps, to set an amount that you will contribute for your room and board.) Between the time that you and your parents set the guidelines and the time that you reach the starting date, you may have certain skills you will want to have learned. You may need to learn how to do your own laundry, for example, or how to take over a share of the household chores without being reminded. If you have not had classes in money management or how to keep a checkbook, these will be important skills to master.

Guidelines for your independence while living at home may include a list of who is responsible for what. Will you be paying for a portion of the household expenses or insurance? How much participation in household chores will be expected of you? Will your school tuition be paid by you or by your parents? What about the cost of books? If your tuition and books are paid by your parents, will they want to keep a close eye on your grades? Together, you and your parents will want to consider these and many other issues. Making decisions on these issues ahead of time will save controversy and conflict later.

Some of the special problems you may encounter and some possible solutions are:

1. You may be so used to being reminded of things you need to do that you may miss important deadlines or appointments; or, conversely, your parents may be so used to reminding you that they continue to do so when you don't need it. You and your

parents might schedule a monthly (or more often) get-together when you look over your progress and discuss any issues that need to be resolved.

2. As you try out independence for the first time, you may find it easy to overextend yourself in terms of commitment of time or money. Spend a little time looking over your budget and your schedule to see how you are doing. Perhaps you can set a specific time every other week or so to do a personal evaluation. If you see signs of trouble, ask for help and guidance.

3. You may feel discouraged from time to time when everything isn't going smoothly. That's normal. One thing we are not prepared for as children is the fact that things aren't automatically perfect and one doesn't automatically know what to do in every situation when one becomes an adult. When you go through a difficult period, work your way out, knowing that things *will* get better, and that you probably won't make the same mistakes again.

Other Special Problems

Your return home may not have affected only you. Perhaps you are one of many who experience a divorce situation with all the legal and financial complications that it can entail. If there are children involved, the problems are even greater. That may be beyond the scope of this book to deal with and may be a situation in which counseling may be especially helpful. You have an attorney to help you with you legal problems, but the complex emotional difficulties associated with divorce and possibly with child custody and visitation issues may need special attention. A trained counselor has seen many people in similar circumstances and can help you distinguish which problems are typical of people in your situation and which are related to your learning disabilities.

Moving On

The temporary return home of the adult with learning disabilities may be a phenomenon of the times rather than a part of the experience of learning disabilities, but the problems often associated with learning disabilities can be prevented from making a temporary arrangement into a permanent situation. With forethought and understanding, it may be a fulfilling and worthwhile experience and an opportunity for closeness the family may otherwise not have had.

How do you know when it's time for you to move on and be completely on your own again? If you set goals for yourself when you return home, either alone or with your parents, knowing when it's time to move on will be an easy matter – that time will be when you have met those goals. It's always easier to know that you have arrived when you know where you are going.

Perhaps your goal was to have completed school or to have found a new job or to have debts paid or a certain amount in savings. When you've reached that point, it might be a good idea to reevaluate your situation. Are there changes that might affect your previously-set plans? Be sure that the costs you counted on for moving out on your own are still realistic. If apartment rents have gone up considerably, or if the roommate you were counting on has decided to get married, you may want to reschedule and reevaluate your moving out date. It's better to be sure you have taken every possible step to ensure the success of this venture than to risk running into more troubles than you can handle.

If your reevaluation shows that your situation is just as you thought it should be, go for it! You'll be doing still more careful planning. Finding a place to live that's convenient to your job or to school, checking on costs, transportation, utilities – you'll be spending quite a bit of time being sure everything is ready before you make your move. This time you know you're going to be successful.

Summary

In this chapter, we have considered living at home with your parents, either after living on your own for a while or staying at home as an adult until you're ready to be independent. Just as nobody asks a graduate how old he or she was at graduation, no one asks how old you were when you moved out on your own, so taking your time and making sure you're ready can be a wise move for an adult with learning disabilities. We've looked at what you and your parents can do to make the experience of living at home as an adult into a positive, growth-producing experience for everyone involved.

Chapter 10

Love and Relationships

Whether it's a close relationship or a romance, a caring relationship is important to everyone. My friends are important to me, and I often realize how much a part of my life they are. Because my schedule is so busy, a telephone call may be the only link between us for weeks at a time. Yet telephone skills are among my poorest because of my auditory learning disabilities!

My auditory memory problems often make me either forget what was said or who told me what because I didn't see the friend I was talking to at the time, and I don't have the visual memory of my friend to help my memory. All I have is my memory of the sound of the person's voice, and for me, that's not good enough!

I also often misunderstand, or am misunderstood, and without the visual cues I use to check my impressions in person, I can get myself into difficulty. Because friendship and relationships are important to me, though, I make every effort to use the telephone, even if it is a difficult tool for me, to maintain contact with those I care about.

Some of us, as people with learning disabilities, often find we have just a few good friends rather than many casual friends. Frequently, those troublesome characteristics that often accompany learning disabilities may make us feel uncomfortable at meeting new people, may make us appear awkward or shy, or, alternatively, may even make us seem too boisterous or outgoing.

Sometimes it's difficult for us to judge how the other person perceives us, and we may think we're being rejected when a new person actually likes us, or we may not catch the cues that should let us know that a person isn't interested. Since forming good relationships is so difficult, keeping the old friends becomes even more important.

How LD/ADD Problems Can Cause Relationship Problems

We can examine some of the problems we might have in forming and maintaining friendships and close relationships and look at some ways of dealing with these problems. Luckily, it's unlikely that any one of us has *all* these characteristics. You may want to go through the list and see which are your particular troubles and think about some of the suggestions for dealing with the possible problems these characteristics may present.

Of course, as with other chapters in this book, there may be some sections that don't pertain to you, or that you don't need. Feel free to look ahead for parts that may be more appropriate for you.

Memory Problems

Since nothing seems to cause trouble in a relationship more than broken promises, those of us with memory problems tend to be in constant hot water because we forget things. We may forget when or where we are to meet a friend, or what we said we would do – or *not* do. We may be boring when we repeat a story we forget we've already told. Or we may be thought unfeeling if we forget something a friend told us.

Memory problems tend to be of particular types. As I have said, I have particular difficulty with auditory memory, or remembering what I hear. I deal with this by writing things down – in fact, there are stacks of paper and pencil holders by all of my telephones, both at home and at the office. I often say that I can't talk on the telephone without pencil and paper. This is because in spite of my ability to *understand* at a high level, I also *forget* very rapidly anything that isn't in a visual form. When this is combined with my difficulty in auditory perception, that is, my ability to discriminate similar things that I hear, it can cause me all sorts of problems.

When I can listen in person, I can focus on the person's face and use the cues I gain there to help structure my memory. If I am only listening on the telephone, I must struggle to make mental pictures or scribble notes to help hold the information in memory. Of course, I don't always do this if the conversation is purely social, and, as a result, I forget a great deal.

As I have been preparing the material for this book, I realized that one reason I may forget whether I have told a particular friend some joke or incident is because often these conversations have taken place on the telephone when I don't have that visual image of my friend to help me remember.

Do you have memory problems that cause difficulties for you in relationships? Think about problems that you have had in the past. Have you often been told, "How could you have forgotten?" or "But you said that you would do such-and-such!" or "I told you about it last week!" If this sounds terribly familiar, then you may need to work out some strategies to help you deal with memory problems. Some of the ideas in Chapter 7, "Around the Home," such as the memo board at home or an appointment book to carry in pocket or purse, may be helpful.

It may also be helpful to figure out whether your visual or your auditory memory is more faulty. If an assessment of your learning patterns has been done, you should have access to that information in the report of your testing. If not, review the checklists included in Chapter 3 for an idea of your learning style. Are you more likely to remember what you see or what you hear? Do you visualize something you want to remember, or do you say it over and over to yourself? Once you know which type of memory is weaker and which is stronger, you can use that information to remind yourself to put information into the form you remember best.

It was a kind of joke in our house – my daughter and I both had serious auditory memory problems, and my husband had poor visual memory. Valerie or I would say, "Have you seen such-and-such?" And he would ask with a grin, "Did it make a noise?" The joke was that if whatever it was *didn't* make a noise, he would not have noticed it at all, much less remembered it! Conversely, he was often astonished that one of us might hear a piece of music a dozen times and not recognize it. We teased that we were lucky because if it was really a nice piece of music, we had the pleasure of hearing it as a new experience many times!

Invading Personal Space

For learning disabled people with visual perceptual problems and body image problems, judging how close to another person one may stand or sit is often difficult. People tend to be comfortable when a certain amount of space exists between them and others – what is called "personal space." Did you ever notice that on a crowded elevator, people may not be uncomfortable standing quite close, but when several people get off, everyone moves apart to allow for more space? Most people are more comfortable standing near family members or people they know quite well. If you, as a stranger, move in too close, the other person may feel very uncomfortable.

If you are not sure if you tend to invade people's space, ask a trusted close friend. If this is a problem for you, try to be more aware of how close you are and try standing back just a bit more.

Inappropriate Touching

Some learning disabled people may have problems with touching other people inappropriately. The person does not intend to be fresh or rude but often is completely unaware of touching the other person. One learning disabled woman finally figured out the reason she so frequently reached out and touched the arm of the person to whom she was speaking. She did it so that she could monitor how close she was standing! She found that many people – especially other learning disabled people – were uncomfortable being touched at all, and most were bothered at the frequency of her touch. She began to make a strong effort to be aware of her touching and use other ways to monitor her closeness.

Inappropriate touching can be an especially bothersome problem for learning disabled women in conversation with men, who may misinterpret the innocent touching as an invitation to more closeness than is intended! Likewise, a man who touches inappropriately may find himself considered "fresh."

Tactile Defensiveness or *Startling Easily*

People who are tactile-defensive don't like to be touched, especially lightly. They may enjoy, for example, holding hands rather firmly or a gripping bear hug. A light touch on the arm to get such a person's attention may result in repulsion or startling. Of course, some of us are also made anxious by being held too tightly. When two people with opposing problems like this get together, it takes willingness to communicate to work out a loving compromise!

A person who startles easily when touched may seem nervous or may overreact, sometimes offending a friend who meant his or her touch to be friendly or reassuring. If you have problems with being touched, it may be important for you to let close friends know that you're not annoyed or angry but that it is just one of the problems associated with your learning disability. Good friends will understand and try to remember to wait for you to invite their touch.

Poor Pressure Monitoring

Some of us may have difficulty judging how hard we hug or shake hands or how heartily we may slap another on the back. If you receive negative reactions from people in these situations, you may want to work with a friend, especially on handshaking. The simplest way to deal with the clap or slap on the back is just not to do it! There's no social situation where it is essential, and too many people find it uncomfortable.

A warm, friendly hug is, to me, one of life's treasures if it's from a friend or loved one. A gripping, too-hard hug or a hug from someone I hardly know is uncomfortable for me. Some men with learning disabilities, especially, seem to have trouble knowing how tightly to hug.

Poor Vocal Loudness Monitoring

A special problem for learning disabled individuals who are more visual in their orientation is difficulty in knowing how loudly to speak for the size of the room, the number of people, or the closeness of the people. One man who loves to tell wonderfully interesting stories often drives away his audience at parties when he speaks because he speaks several levels louder than the others in the group. Of course, speaking too loudly is often a symptom of hearing loss, and if you have trouble monitoring your vocal loudness, you should certainly consider having your hearing checked.

To work on cultivating a comfortable degree of vocal loudness, practice with a friend and concentrate on the *feeling* of your voice at a particular loudness. When you speak too softly, someone is always willing to tell you to speak up, but people usually are not comfortable in telling someone to speak more softly!

Verbal Impulsivity

Just saying whatever pops into mind is a problem for many of us. When a young child loudly remarks, "Boy, is that lady fat!" people (except for the child's mother and the large lady!) tend to be amused. When the impulsive speaker is an adult, the situation is not funny. Often, the LD/ADD adult may make a comment intended only for a companion to hear but may not be aware he or she is speaking loudly enough to be overheard by others. A friend or relative can tell you if you make such remarks and probably be glad you asked. Those who have problems in the area often embarrass their friends as well as themselves.

Verbal impulsivity can also involve speaking angrily at the least provocation. Angry words are always difficult to take back and often impossible to erase. When one has difficulty in understanding spoken words and in interpreting tone of voice as well as verbal impulsivity, there is the constant risk of being offended over nothing and creating a situation that is now a *real* problem. This problem can cause major difficulties in the work situation as well as in social situations.

Dealing with verbal impulsivity is difficult, for it means guarding your tongue much of the time. Getting into the habit of waiting before you speak is a hard task, but worth the effort. If you find you often get in trouble for angry remarks because you took offense at something that wasn't intended, work on asking for clarification. Try something simple, such as "I'm sorry, I'm not sure I understand. What did you mean?" when you think someone has insulted you. Often, you'll find the remark was not at all what you thought!

Physical Impulsivity

We're all familiar with children's physical impulsivity to such an extent that most adults automatically step on the brakes when a ball rolls into the street, fully expecting a child to come dashing after it without looking. LD/ADD adults with physical impulsivity problems often seem clumsy because their unthinking actions frequently result in spills, drops, and knockovers.

I think I became most aware of how much of a problem we LD people have with physical impulsivity when I attended meetings of the National Network of Learning Disabled Adults. During one day's meeting, three pitchers of water were spilled.

Nobody seemed upset; it was such a common thing to happen that each time, someone just put a stack of napkins on the spill and went right on talking!

Generally, the impulsive adult is responding to one stimulus without being able to deal with all the other factors involved. It's not a problem that's easy to deal with except in the home environment where the key is keeping things simple and uncluttered so that when impulsive movement *does* occur, there's less in the way to provide barriers.

Misinterpretation of Facial Expression

Many adults with problems in this area get into difficulty because they are unable to pick up the signs others give in social situations. For example, a slight frown or tightening of the lips may indicate that the listener is offended by an off-color story, or by a speaker's using a supervisor or customer's first name without invitation. A smile and tilt of the head may mean that a listener is interested in getting to know the speaker better, but the ADD/LD adult may miss those signs. Working with a friend or a group, such as a support group or self-help organization, in learning to watch for such communication can be helpful.

Misinterpretation of Vocal Tone

For those of us with auditory problems, slight differences in tone of voice or in phrasing may signal reactions that we miss until too late, one reason I find telephone communication so difficult – without the visual information I get from facial expressions, I have difficulty knowing how I am being received by the other person when I can only hear the voice. I try to deal with the problem by asking for feedback when I am unsure of how well I am communicating. As with interpretation of tone of voice, this is a good skill to work on with a friend or a group.

Misinterpretation of Body Language

Many books and articles on body language, suggest that it is almost a rather precise form of communication. I don't think that's so! Crossed arms may mean that a person doesn't want to listen or it may mean that he or she is simply chilly. Some things, though, are very obvious to most people unless their LD or ADD-related problems get in the way. For example, when a person keeps backing away, sometimes a person with problems in this area doesn't realize it means that he or she has been moving in too close. What frequently happens then is that the other person moves away, only to be followed, until the other person becomes so uncomfortable he or she ends the conversation. The LD adult may feel hurt and bewildered and never know what happened.

Misinterpretation of Social Situations

Perhaps one of the most common problems in this area is knowing when to leave during a visit or when to end a telephone call. One man with this problem used to tell me about wonderful job interviews he had that lasted for hours, after which he promptly got letters informing him that he did not get the job. During one social visit, he had far overstayed his welcome and had missed so many of my subtle hints that it was time for him to go home, I finally had to ask him to leave. Suddenly I realized that he had probably had the same problem in the interviews, overstaying so long that even if he had already made a good impression, he lost it by not knowing when to leave.

Literalness

Interpreting everything according to the exact wording, without awareness of common expressions used in fun or as figures of speech, is called *literalness.* For example, a learning disabled woman studying child development heard the instructor refer to a child's "arrested development" and thought that the child had stopped growing because he had been arrested by the police!

Most people who have this problem, however, do not have it to this degree. Some may simply be slow to react as they go over a statement mentally and discover that it was not meant literally but was spoken in fun or had another meaning. Some of us, though, have many problems in interpreting teasing remarks, taking things seriously that were said in a tone of voice that most people would understand actually meant the opposite.

Disorganization

Being organized is very difficult for most of us with learning disabilities. Even though many of us need good organization in order to cope with our lives, it is often the most difficult skill we have to master. For example, when I get very rushed, I often tell myself, "I don't have time to put that where it belongs! I'll do it later." Then, of course, what happens is that so many things get piled up out of order, I can't find them when I need them and can't find the time to take on what has now become a very big job of trying to get organized. This is a skill I'm still working on.

Some people with learning disabilities find that being well organized is what has saved them the most trouble in their home and work lives. You may think that being disorganized or messy affects only you, but in a relationship it ends up affecting everyone.

As you work toward becoming better organized, you may find that it helps you deal with some of your other problems as well. For example, you don't have to worry so much about using your poor memory to help you remember where you put something if you have a system and always put things away in the same place. I don't have to hunt for my bills when it is time to pay them because as I go through the mail each day, all the bills go into one basket until payday. Then they are all in one place, and I don't have to spend time looking for them.

For some hints on organization, take a look at some of the ideas in Chapter 7, "Around the House." The books suggested at the end of that chapter may also be useful.

Overactivity

Overactivity, sometimes called *hyperactivity*, is excessive movement. Some overactive adults can't stay at one activity for long; some can't sit still even when they are sitting but are constantly jiggling a foot or squirming in their chairs. In recent years, medications such as Ritalin commonly used for hyperactive children have begun to be used with adults as well. It might be useful to consult your doctor if you feel that your activity level is a problem for you or the people in your life.

Meeting People

Single people of all ages, not just people with learning disabilities, seem to be always looking for ways to meet people, especially of the opposite sex. Going places and doing things alone just isn't always fun. Human beings are creatures who tend to enjoy the company of others, and sometimes more than two makes a crowd. It's fun to have someone special to share big and little events of the day with, to go places with, and just to be with when you need a special friend.

Because of some of the problems we've discussed that learning disabled people have in addition to the problems with learning, meeting new people may be difficult. How to form real and lasting friendships and relationships when we *do* meet new people can be even harder.

Where do you meet new people? For most of our lives, we met people mostly at school. As an adult, your life may or may not include school. So where now?

On the job, at the office, or wherever the workplace may be is one place where you are likely to meet others with similar interests. Of course, people you work with will have some interests similar to yours, but one problem may be that many business settings discourage people who work together from dating. Often it causes problems if one is promoted to a supervisory position and then is in a position of authority over the other. Also, when a couple breaks up or has a disagreement, the problems can spill over to the job.

A church or synagogue is a good place to meet people. If you already attend services regularly, you might want to inquire about programs you may not have known about. There may be study groups or singles groups or even age-level social groups you might enjoy. You'll find that such groups are always happy to hear from new people interested in joining.

Even if you not a regular at services, you might think about going for a while. First of all, you can be sure of a welcome. You can usually attend services a time or two without being overwhelmed by too many people, but most congregations now have welcoming committees or cards in a display case that you can sign to have someone contact you about the different programs you might be interested in.

One especially good way to meet people is to volunteer to help with one of the programs for people in your age or interest group. There are never enough volunteers for the jobs that need doing, and you will meet many more people than if you just go to services or to meetings. Be sure, of course, that you volunteer for a job in an area you are strong in. Don't volunteer to write up notices for the newspaper unless you're a good writer. If you have good telephone skills, volunteering for the telephone committee would be a better choice for you.

Clubs, such as hobby clubs, can also be good social outlets. If you are in or near a city, there will be many groups for a variety of interests – garden clubs, amateur radio, biking or walking groups – almost any special interest will have a formal or informal group meeting with some degree of regularity. Good sources of information are the public library's information desk or your local newspaper.

Volunteering for certain jobs in a club can help you meet people, just as they can in your synagogue or church group. Helping call people with announcements about meetings is a great way to get to talk to people and learn their names. Then, when you encounter them at meetings, you already have a good way to start your first conversation: "Hi, I'm Jim. I'm the one who called you about the meeting. It's nice to meet you in person!" Another good job is the welcoming committee or giving out name tags. You'll get to meet everyone who comes to the meeting, and everyone will know your name!

Dating

In years gone by, dating was mostly thought of as concerning teenagers and people in their twenties. Other people were either too young to date, were married or had settled on being single. Oh, of course, there were others who went out on dates, but the rituals and language of dating were mostly reserved for the high schoolers and college-age group. Now the rules and age limits have changed a great deal. A woman can invite a man out; either one may pay; a woman may even send flowers to a man after a date!

Many of the concerns about dating that a person with learning disabilities might have are the same concerns as with any relationship. Meeting people, hoping they like you, getting along, understanding verbal and non-verbal signals from one another – these are some issues that everyone faces. For the person with learning disabilities, taking another close look at the problem areas above can be very helpful. Which of the problems described above are yours? Are you working on eliminating them as much as possible or figuring out strategies for dealing with them?

Using some of the strategies presented above to help you meet people is a good beginning. If you meet someone you'd like to go out with, you can take the step of simply inviting the person to go to dinner or a movie with you. If you're a man, this is fairly routine. If you're a woman, you may do the same, or you may give the man your telephone number and suggest he call you sometime.

If you're shy about calling someone for a date, sometimes it helps to remember that the worst thing that can happen is that the person may say, "No." Then again, the answer may be, "Yes, I'd love to!" So there's not much to lose. Think of an activity you'd enjoy, check on the day and time that would be good, and make that call. Of course, if it's a concert or play when there is a chance that tickets may be sold out, you may want to check in advance to be sure that tickets are still available and their price.

Some people with learning disabilities make notes before calling to ask someone out. It's not a bad idea! You might want to note the things you want to be sure to work out: The activity, the day, the time of the activity, and what time you will pick up your date, if that's the plan.

Severe learning disabilities have caused some people to decide that it takes so much time and effort to cope with the demands of job and life, there is little emotional strength left to cope with a close relationship. For them, living alone, sharing holidays and special times with relatives and friends, and maintaining a good professional life is enough. Others may continue to try to find that special someone to share their lives in spite of problems and frustrations.

If one-to-one relationships have been difficult for you, it may be time to think about counseling to help you identify what the problems might have been that have gotten in the way. You may find that you have been picking the wrong kind of person rather than having behaviors you particularly need to change. Or you may find that problems unrelated to your learning disability are interfering. In any case, a good counselor can help you seek some answers.

Counseling can also help if you are in a relationship that has problems. While marriage counseling is for married couples, more counselors and therapists are now doing relationship counseling for couples who are not married and who may or may not be thinking of marrying, but who have a long-term or serious relationship they would like to maintain.

Talking About Your Learning Disability

Perhaps one of the most important aspects of a relationship is communication, and one of the ways a relationship can break down the fastest is when there is not enough communication. It may be important for your "significant other" (the person with whom you have that very important love relationship) to know from the beginning that you have certain problems that may affect both of you. It may not be something you tell everyone you go out with, but as it begins to look as if "this is the one" person who is going to be special to you, the sooner you talk about your learning problems, the better.

You may want to talk about some of the problems covered in the first part of this chapter, and perhaps even let your significant other read the book. The two of you may need to work out ways to deal with some of the problems so that they won't turn your special times together into troubled times. For example, some couples have signals they use with each other so that they can avoid conflict.

One hyperactive man who had trouble with his behavior when he got restless at parties would signal his girlfriend with a gesture that is familiar even to people without learning problems. He would let her know he had spent about as much time at the party as he could handle by tapping his watch. She would know they needed to leave soon. Also, when he was talking too loudly, a problem he often had, she would place one hand over her ear.

You may want to develop some signs or signals you and your special person can use, too. For example, if your significant other is aware that you often invade other people's personal space, he or she can hold your arm or pat your back as a signal for you to move away.

There may be other problems that can be handled by a caring friend, too. If you tend to be awkward or clumsy in crowded settings, you may agree in advance that you won't be the one to carry the drinks or the plates at a buffet dinner!

Intimacy and Sex

Emotional closeness to a significant other may lead to a decision to be close physically as well. For some people, even with today's relaxed attitudes about sex, physical intimacy and closeness is for the marriage relationship only. For others, it is a natural part of a relationship that may have less long-term commitment.

That decision is one that should be made by you and your significant other. If sex will be part of your relationship, it *should be a decision*, not just an impulsive act or something one or the other agrees to in order not to lose the relationship.

Intimacy is more than just having sex. Intimacy is sharing feelings and caring about the other person. If a relationship doesn't include that kind of sharing and caring, sex will not improve it; it will only make the problems deeper. Spend time getting to know your significant other before making a decision to have sex. Is this a person you care about, and who cares about you? Are there trust and honesty in the relationship?

If the decision is that you and your partner will have sex, one thing that should *not* be a matter of choice is whether or not you will practice safe sex. It should be a rule, absolutely, that every time you have sex, a condom made of latex should be used. The threat of various sexually transmitted diseases in the past was that a person might become infected and have to be treated. For AIDS, however, there is no cure. AIDS is fatal. In spite of all the rumors of ways you might get AIDS, there are certain things we know for sure: One way you can get AIDS is through unprotected sex.

182

Using a condom does not guarantee that you won't get AIDS because a condom can break, but so far, it is the best protection available other than just not having sex.

If you have questions about the danger of AIDS, talk to your doctor, or, if you feel uncomfortable about asking him or her, check the telephone directory for an AIDS information center that you can call for information. It's your life we are talking about, so don't take chances with this one. Remember, use a latex condom, *every time.*

Communication

Throughout this chapter, I have referred over and over to the importance of talking to a trusted friend or relative if you are not sure you have some of the characteristics we have been discussing. As you can see, I consider honest, open communication to be very important. Often, we cannot clearly see ourselves and our little defects. It is sad to hear someone say, "I would have changed if I had known you hated that!" It almost always means that someone was really bothered by something another person was doing but didn't speak up about it.

Now, change is hard, and annoying habits aren't going to go away in an instant. Sometimes we forget, and sometimes old habits are just too hard to break. It takes time! For example, a good friend of mine is a wonderful joke-teller. Unfortunately, he often makes jokes at lunch. I tend to get upset when someone tells what I call "yucky jokes" (jokes about unpleasant subjects) at mealtime. I have asked him many times not to, but because of his ADD problems with impulsivity, he often forgets. We've agreed that I'll stop him if it looks like the subject is going in that direction. He hasn't stopped altogether, but he's getting better!

And perhaps that's the secret. Because we're good friends, and our friendship is important to both of us, we're willing to work on the problem. He's willing to try to stop doing something that really bothers me, I'm willing to be patient and try to help him stop, and we're both willing to try not to get angry at each other about it!

In all close relationships, whether with a friend, a significant other, or a family member, the ability to talk openly about facts and feelings, and the ability to separate the two, is important. How you deliver the message can be the key. For example, suppose I say to a friend, "You are always late. I don't care if it is one of your LD problems. I'm sick of it! I'd like to get some place on time for a change!" How long do you think the relationship will last? Probably not very long. But suppose instead I say, "I really am bothered by being late. How can I help you so that we can be on time? Would you like me to call you about an hour before you are going to pick me up to remind you?" What was important here was that I started out by telling my friend how I felt and offered a suggestion about what I would be willing to do rather than just criticizing him and indicating I didn't care.

Now, nobody's perfect although I wish I could tell you that I am. Sometimes I forget, and we may fight over some really small issue. Because we are friends, though, one of us, and sometimes both of us, will apologize later. That's an important part of a good relationship, too – being able to have a disagreement or even an unreasonable fight, yet being able to make up later.

Fighting Fair

I used to think that "fighting fair" was a silly idea. The idea of a fight, I thought, was that you wanted to win, whatever the cost. Now I think that it is important to think about what you want in the long run. Most of the time, we want to continue the relationship, but with something changed. Usually, if we have decided that a relationship isn't worth keeping, it's just not worth fighting over, and we might be able just to walk away.

If we want to keep the relationship, though, there are some rules for fighting fair that can help. Here are some of them:

184

Stick to the point. If this is a fight about someone forgetting to do something he or she promised, fight about that, and not about another problem or another event. Bringing up every little thing that ever happened, now or earlier, will make the fight last longer, but it won't solve the problem you're facing now.

Don't insult each other. A fight should be about what happened, not about personal characteristics. If he left you waiting when he was supposed to pick you up after work, say, "I felt stupid waiting and waiting! I am really mad!" not "You stupid, insensitive clod! You don't care about me!"

Don't say things you can never take back. This is a very important rule for fighting fair – maybe the most important one of all. When we were children, we believed that words could be taken back. There are some things, though, that can never be taken back and never should be said. "I never really liked you! I just started going with you because I felt sorry for you!" is a remark that will hurt and never go away. Personal, cruel remarks about someone's appearance are permanently hurtful, too.

Say what you'd like to have happen. Sometimes fights go on and on because nobody will say what he or she would like the outcome to be. "I just want us to have one time a week when we sit and talk instead of watching sports on TV!" is more likely to get results than, "All you ever do is come over here and watch sports on TV!"

Remember to be willing to say "I'm sorry" and mean it. Even when the fight is over, it's hard to lose the bad feeling that may have come up. One good way to help them go away is to say, "I'm sorry." That means not following it with something like,". . . but you really made me mad!" or any other comment that might start the fight going again. It especially helps if you can follow "I'm sorry" with a loving remark, such as "I'm willing to try harder" or just "I really care about you, and I'm glad we're not fighting now."

Try to settle the problem before the fight starts. This may be the best advice of all, especially for those of us with learning disabilities. It's hard for us to remember rules, and we sometimes impulsively say or do the wrong things. Experts used to say that fighting, as long as it was fair fighting, was good for relationships. Now some experts are suggesting that fighting just leads people to fight more and stay angry with each other. Communicating with each other *before* it gets to the fight stage may save many heartaches.

Summary

Relationships, whether with friends or significant others, are an important part of life. Relationships may not be as romantic as in the movies, but life isn't a movie! The social situations, friendships, and romantic relationships we want as people with learning disabilities are no different than those of our non-learning disabled friends.

As learning disabled people, though, there are many different social situations in which we may have difficulty. Some of the things we may experience and some possible solutions have been discussed in this chapter.

You may want to review the checklists in Chapter 3, as suggested in this chapter, and you may want to read the next chapter, "Marriage and Family Life," even if you aren't married. There are more hints that may help you, even in relationships with friends and co-workers.

Chapter 11

Marriage and Family Life

Marriage and family life can be wonderful or terrible, fulfilling or distressing, warm and loving or cold and destructive – the possibilities are endless! Of course, what everyone wants is to have all of the good things and to avoid all of the bad. It's not always possible even in the best of marriages and most loving of families for things to go smoothly all the time. Perhaps it's how we handle the bad times that is the real test of a marriage and family.

A person with learning disabilities has some added problems to face in working for a successful marriage or in living as a part of a family. Whether you are an adult still living with your parents, a person who has decided not to marry, already married (with or without children), or just beginning to think about the problems and promise of marriage and family life, some of the issues we will look at in this chapter will be important to you. Just as with earlier chapters, you can pick and choose the parts that may be helpful in your situation. Feel free to skip ahead if there are parts that do not apply to your life and family setting.

If You're Already Married

Perhaps you have been married for some time – maybe even for many years and have a family – and are concerned about how your learning disability may be affecting your spouse and your children. Whether you've known about the learning disability for a long time or are just discovering it, you may want to do some careful thinking about some of the problems that were presented in Chapter 10, "Love and Relationships." You and your spouse may want to sit down and honestly discuss each of the possible problems described.

One way you might approach the subject is to mark the problems you think you have and ask your spouse to look over the list, marking any others he or she thinks might be causing you trouble. Then the two of you can discuss them and try to explore ways to make them less of a problem in your marriage.

I recently talked with the wife of a man with learning disabilities who said, "I'm tired of always having to be the one who does the reminding. We have the work divided, but nothing gets done unless I keep track of it!" Her husband agreed that he forgot often but stressed that he was always willing to do what he had agreed when reminded as long as it was just a reminder and not an angry fight. How many times I have heard those same complaints from *non*-learning disabled people!

In this case, however, I asked how the household chores were divided – traditionally, with old-fashioned notions of men and women's jobs? According to interest? Or according to the abilities or disabilities of the two? I was assured that the chores were divided according to the abilities of each spouse. He was a better cook, but she did the shopping and kitchen clean-up. He vacuumed and dusted; she did the laundry. He made the beds; she cleaned the bathrooms. He mowed the lawn; she did the edging and trimmed the hedge. He kept the budget and checkbook up to date; she wrote the checks and mailed everything.

I suggested that they consider the "job of reminding" simply one more of the household tasks to be assigned to the person best able to do it. It really didn't change what needed to be done, or who was to do it, but the difference in the couple's feelings about the situation changed almost at once!

Traditional roles may not fit.

A friend of mine once said that he thought the perfect wife would be a friend, lover, sister, mother, and maybe even daughter, although not always at the same time. Sometimes, he said, he would want his wife just to be his best friend. Other times, his lover. Sometimes he would want her to be more like a sister – family, but different from wife or mother. Sometimes he'd feel like a little boy who would want his wife to act like a mother and comfort him. At still other times he'd want to feel like the father who was comforting *her*. And, yes, he said he'd be willing to be friend, lover, brother, son, or father to her, depending on their needs at different times.

I think that what my friend was saying is important. It may not be possible to be the traditional *anything* any more, and maybe the traditions were only myths.

We used to think that the husband earned the money and made the decisions but did nothing around the house except mowed the lawn, worked on the car, or perhaps took out the garbage. The wife stayed home, cooked and cleaned, did the shopping, and handled all the child care. Maybe we were wrong and were just fooled by the picture of family life we saw in movies or on television. Maybe in the past there were more women who changed the oil in the family car, and more men who ironed the daughters' dresses than we thought. Today, though, we know that more and more people are coming to believe that following traditional roles is not always the best approach in their particular families.

In a family in which one or more member have learning disabilities, it is especially important to be flexible about roles. Who does which job may have to be decided based on who is most able to do that particular job. Then the other spouse may have to take on a different task so that the work is shared.

We may also have to develop new ideas about what is fair. Sometimes it will not be possible to divide up the jobs so that each person does exactly half, or so that the hours of work divide evenly. For a parent with learning disabilities, sometimes the stress of the job is so great that a little time alone without responsibilities at the end of the work day may be absolutely necessary. That may mean that the other parent, who might also like a few minutes of peace, may have to take on the parenting duties alone for a while.

Creative ideas may help, too. Perhaps a carefully chosen children's videotape that the children may watch for the first half hour after everyone arrives home may be a good solution. A snack of fresh vegetables cut in finger-size pieces and served with dip may keep young appetites in check while parents get themselves together and relax or begin dinner preparations. Even parents who would like to limit their children's television viewing may find that just a short segment each evening of a good children's videotape may be acceptable and will give everyone in the family a chance to settle down just a little.

Sharing the Work

Who fixes dinner and who supervises the children's homework or bedtime preparations may need to be decided on a non-traditional basis. One learning disabled couple found that the mother was far too stressed in the evening to be relaxed with the children but was always much more cheerful than the father in the morning. The two of them simply divided up the jobs of supervising the children according to the time of day. While the father handled supervision of the children in the evening, the mother took on all the evening kitchen chores. In the morning, the mother handled child supervision while the father fixed breakfast and made sack lunches for everyone.

Other household jobs may be divided by abilities, too. How I'd love to have someone handle all my telephone jobs! I hate having to call the plumber or make arragements by telephone. I don't mind running errands, though, and I'm very organized at getting ten or more errands done on one outing. A couple can sit down together over a cup of coffee and look at the family jobs, dividing them up according to ability. Of course, there may be a few jobs that neither one wants! These should be shared or divided so that one person doesn't get *all* the unpleasant jobs that either one might have been able to do. Some of the same ideas in Chapter 7, "Around the House," may help in deciding who does which jobs.

Considering Marriage

Some learning disabled people simply decide that marriage is too complicated and too difficult. I don't know of any statistics that tell how many of us make that decision. I also don't know how many of us get married, *then* find out how hard it can be, and get divorced. Many, many marriages of non-learning disabled people also end in divorce, so I would not want to suggest that learning disabilities cause divorce; however, I do know that people with learning disabilities often attribute their failures in marriage and relationships to their learning problems.

Some spouses of people with learning disabilities, too, have felt that the learning disability was the cause of the divorce. And in some marriages where *both* the spouse had learning disabilities, problems sometimes became overwhelming.

In considering marriage, it will be important for a couple to be open and honest about the learning disabilities and the problems they involve. That's sometimes hard to do when a couple is thinking only about love and being together. Still, because they *are* in love and want to *stay* together, they can prevent many problems from coming up by planning together.

Chapter 10, "Love and Relationships," discussed some of the important problems that might cause difficulties for a couple. For a couple considering marriage and possibly children, it will be important to look at *all* of the problems of learning disability. This means looking at the academic problems, not just the social ones. If the person with the learning disability is a non-reader or writer, this means that all of the family duties involving these tasks will fall to the future spouse who *can* read or write. If the learning disability has limited the person's education or the kinds of jobs he or she is able to hold, both parties must be sure that

191

they understand what this means in terms of their future family income and responsibilities.

As I have said several times in this book, sometimes it's a good idea to involve someone else in these discussions. I know that many people feel that these are decisions that they want to make themselves, and I agree! I feel, however, that a good counselor can help an individual or a couple sort out all of the things that they will want to consider to help them make the right decision.

What is important here is that both parties know and think as much as possible about the marriage responsibilities in advance. Often in life we have trouble dealing with things only because we didn't know about them ahead of time. Of course, sometimes we find we can't do something we thought we would be able to do, but knowing ahead of time makes it easier to give our best effort. It also means that there is time to be sure that we are *willing* to give our best effort, too.

What if both of you have learning disabilities?

If both of the couple have learning disabilities, one thing that will not be a problem is knowing how it feels! Unfortunately, however, this does not mean that it's automatically going to be easy to be understanding. Sometimes people who need patience and understanding the most are the least patient and the least understanding of others!

Working out strategies for dealing with your strengths and weaknesses can help. How lucky it would be if one of you had strengths wherever the other had weaknesses! This just doesn't always happen, and you will have to work out creative ways to solve some of your problems. For example, if neither of you reads well, then you may have to arrange for a friend to assist you with written material, such as letters or bills. If you both have trouble with math, particularly the math that is involved in budgeting or keeping household accounts, then you may have to arrange to hire someone to help.

Sometimes people with learning disabilities or ADD cope with their surroundings in different ways or organize things differently. One learning disabled couple had problems when they were first married. Because neither of them had problems in reading, they had many books. The husband wanted the books arranged according to topic but in no particular order otherwise. His wife felt his way of organizing them wasn't organized at all. She wanted all the books arranged alphabetically according to the first word of the title. They finally had to divide the books with hers arranged her way and his arranged his way. Their problem then was to decide what to do when they began to have books that belonged to both of them!

Another couple had trouble dealing with their ADD problems in a way that suited both of them. The wife needed music to shut out the distraction of outside noises and to lull her to sleep at night. Her husband found the music itself distracting, and it kept him awake. They finally compromised by getting her a pillow speaker, a small device that she could plug into her radio and slip under her pillow so that only she could hear the music.

Considering Having Children

Whether or not to have children is a very personal decision for a couple to make. How do we feel about parenting? Do both of us want children? How many children do we want? Are we able to provide for our children in the way that we would like? Do we have the patience and strength to be good parents? These are some of the questions that all couples ask as they think about having children.

If one or both of the couple have learning disabilities, some of these questions may take on even more importance. We know from our experiences that coping with learning disabilities is often stressful and difficult. It can be exhausting. The additional responsibility for caring for the growth and development of children can add even more stress, even for the most patient, calm, even-tempered person. For some of us, it may be very difficult indeed. I know of more than one couple in which one or both had learning disabilities who were able to have good, supportive marriages until they decided to have children. Then they found that the added responsibilities and stress were too much for the marriage.

Children are a wonderful part of family life for most of us. Because you want your children to be happy and well-adjusted and because you want your marriage to continue to do well, you will want to be sure that the two of you can provide the kind of support to each other and the children that will make your family work.

Suppose one or more of the children have learning disabilities?

As we discussed in Chapter 1, we don't have all the answers about learning disabilities. We often don't know what caused a particular person's learning disability. We do know that some kinds of learning disability seem to run in families. As I said in that chapter, sometimes parents only discover their own learning disabilities when they begin to get help for the learning disabilities of their children – in fact, that's how I discovered my own auditory learning problems.

Some of the people reading this book will have had the same experience. They will have been worried about a son or daughter's problems in school, discovered that the problems were caused by a learning disability, and finally found that their own problems years before in school were caused by the same kinds of learning disabilities.

Some of you, however, will have known about your own learning disability but never thought until now that your children might have the same problems. If that's your case, don't waste time worrying about it! First, look at how your children are doing in school and at home. If they are having problems, then the first

194

step is to contact the school and ask for an evaluation. You can let the school know that part of the reason for your concern is your own learning disability, if you like, or you may simply talk about your son or daughter's problems. There is far more help available today than when you were in school, even if that was only a few years ago.

Helping your child understand his or her learning disability may be easier in some ways than it is for parents who have not had learning disabilities themselves. I recommend that you use my book, *The Tuned-In, Turned-On Book About Learning Problems,* which was specially written to help youngsters with learning disabilities understand their problems. It is available from Academic Therapy Publications, the publishers of this book. It is available in both book and audio cassette tape form.

You might want to read the book with your child or listen to the tape together. Some parents have found it helpful to play the tape and follow along in the book. Except for a small part that I read and my daughter's introduction, the tape was done by some wonderful young actors at the Dallas Teen and Children's Theatre, so your child will find the voices easy to listen to and not at all like parents or teachers' voices.

If you have children who do not have learning disabilities, you may want to help them understand your learning disabled child better. For very young children, Joe Lasker's *He's My Brother* tells a story in simple words with lovely pictures of three children, one of whom has learning problems and ADD. Upper elementary and middle school children can relate to Jamie Gilson's *Do Bananas Chew Gum?* A useful book written by a medical doctor, Matthew Galvin, is *Otto Learns About His Medicine: A Story About Medication for Hyperactive Children.* These books are listed in the bibliography at the end of this book.

What if you don't yet have children and are worried that you might pass your learning problems on to any future children you might have? I remember a letter I received several years ago from a young woman who had been misdiagnosed as having other, more severe problems before it was discovered that she had learning disabilities. She was concerned that she might pass on her learning disabilities to her children. She wrote to me several times, beginning when she was in high school. Finally she wrote to me quite proudly to let me know that she was graduating from nursing school! She finally decided that she wanted to have children because she had managed to overcome her learning disabilities and felt confident that she could help her children if they should need it.

To explore the possibility that your learning disability might be one of the types that we suspect can be passed on, you might want to talk to your doctor. Most of the time, of course, we can't be sure. I suspect that if one of your parents or other family members do not have learning disabilities, you are unlikely to pass yours on to your children. Still, you will feel better if you talk to your doctor. If it is appropriate, he or she can send you to a genetic counselor, a specialist who can help you look at your family history to examine the chances that your learning disability might be inherited.

If your child does have learning disabilities, whether similar to your own or different, you will certainly have the advantage over many other parents in your ability to understand what your youngster is going through in the school setting. You will want to seek the appropriate help for your child in school and be supportive of the child's program.

Whether or not you received special help in school for your problems, you may need to consider how you feel about the way your school approached your needs and to think about how those feelings may affect your working with your child's school.

For example, if you received excellent help for your learning disabilities while you were in school, you might assume that your child will, too. While we certainly can hope that this will be so, it is not necessarily going to happen. You will need to work *with* the school and continue to keep track of how your child's needs are being met.

On the other hand, if your own school experiences were not good, and you received little help or inadequate help, you may have a tendency to be negative about the school's attempts to provide a good program for your child. You may need to recognize that services have continued to improve, and that a wider range of types of services is available than ever before. Your child may receive the kind of help that was not even dreamed of when you were in school.

You will want to take an active role with your child's program. Meet with the teachers, attend the meetings, ask questions, and, especially, know your child's rights for services. Your child's school must provide you with a booklet with all the rights to education carefully explained. We all want to be sure our children have every opportunity to succeed, and you can do that by being involved.

Dealing with Children's Questions About a Parent's Learning Disability

If you have children, you know that they can come up with amazing, often embarrassing questions – and often at the most inappropriate times! Even if a parent prepares carefully for explaining where babies come from, the question probably won't be asked at a quiet bedtime or over milk and cookies at the kitchen table. It will probably be asked loudly in the checkout line at the grocery store while you're standing behind a very pregnant woman!

And so it may be with questions about a parent's learning disability. Your child may ask you in front of the person you'd least like to know about it! By letting your child know you, strengths, weaknesses, and all, you have a chance to present the information in a comfortable way on your own terms.

Some parents have tried to hide their learning disabilities from their children. More than once I have heard stories about a parent who pretended not to be interested in helping a child with homework so that he need not let the child know that he could not read. Unfortunately, what usually happens is that the child begins

197

to believe that the parent doesn't care about his or her schoolwork, or, worse still, that the parent is disinterested in the child, a situation that certainly no parent wants.

I am a believer in honesty, as you have been able to tell from all of the earlier chapters in this book. It is important to let your children know your strengths and weaknesses as well as how you cope with your problems. I have often said that one of the things we fail to prepare our children for is the fact that when one becomes an adult, one doesn't automatically know what to do in every situation. It can be helpful, too, for our children to know that we have differences, and that we can learn to live with them and even to overcome them.

With a young child, perhaps only severe learning disabilities may need an explanation. A parent who does not read may look at picture books with a child and tell the story the pictures suggest. Moving to a book with printed text, the parent may simply explain that he or she is not able to read, but that the other parent will read to the child. It may be prudent to say at this point that when the child is older, he or she will be able to read and may even read to the parent.

An older child will need more specific information and an opportunity to ask questions. He or she may benefit from trying some of the simulations of learning disability set forth in Chapter 4. A third or fourth grader would enjoy trying to read "The Story of the Three Little Pigs," which is given without vowels, or "Three Billy Goats Gruff," which is printed backwards. He or she could then understand better how hard it is for Mom or Dad to read. Trying the mirror tracing activity could help a child understand the difficulties of a parent with a severe writing problem or problems with eye-hand coordination.

The child who wonders, "Will I have these problems, too?"should be given as much information as you have at the time. If the child shows normal ability in the areas of the parent's learning disability, then he or she may be assured that there is no problem and be given specific examples to help the child understand. For example, a child might be told, "Yes, Mommy has a problem in reading, but you already are learning to read in school, and you're doing just fine!"

If the child is too young for the evidence to be clear, the youngster may be assured that if there is a problem, he or she will be helped to learn to deal with it. Then the child's strengths should be pointed out.

My granddaughter is aware of her mother and grandmother's learning disabilities, and she has enjoyed our stories of how we watched her early learning to see if the same patterns existed. We point out to her the strengths she has that we do not have, and we delight in her abilities. Had she had our learning disability, we would have praised her efforts to overcome it just as I express my pride in all that my daughter has accomplished in spite of her learning disability.

The important thing to remember is to communicate to the child the information about the disability openly and without embarrassment. Your child can be proud of what you have been able to achieve and can learn much from seeing your willingness to figure out different, often creative ways to be successful.

Other Kinds of Families

We've already discussed the fact that the old ideas about who played which role in the family have changed. It's also true that families can take many different forms. The single-parent family is now very common. If you are a parent raising your child or children alone, you know that there are both joys and difficulties. Whether the children's other parent is involved in their lives or not, you and your children are a family just as much as a two-parent family is.

Perhaps one of the most difficult jobs in a one-parent family is organizing and scheduling so that everything gets done. Unfortunately, organization is often one of the biggest problems for people with learning disabilities. To survive and thrive as a single parent, you may have to think carefully about your priorities. What is really important, and what are some of the things you'd *like* to do, but which can be eliminated?

As a single parent, spending time with your children is probably one of your priorities. Quick, simple meals, often using packaged or frozen foods, may enable you to spend some of the evening time with your children in leisure activities or supervising their homework. A spotless kitchen floor may be less important than watching a son or daughter play T-ball or soccer. When there's not time to do everything, plan to do the things that are most important to all of you as a family.

Sometimes single parents feel guilty that they are not providing as good a childhood for their children as they could if they lived in a two-parent home. Such parents sometimes work desperately to give the children too much and to do too much for them. As a result, they may wear themselves out and spoil their children. Certainly, you do not want your children to grow up expecting to have everything done for them. You want them to grow into independent, capable adults who are able to provide for themselves and who have healthy self-concepts.

Involving your children in household chores rather than trying to do it all yourself is a good way to help them learn to be contributing members of a family. You don't need to feel that you are not doing all you should do as a parent. Children who grow up with real, useful chores that benefit their families from an early age learn to be responsible adults.

There are other kinds of families that are not like traditional father-mother-children families. Being a husband or wife and perhaps a father or mother may not be right for every person with a learning disability. For some, remaining unmarried, but living a fulfilling adult life is a better choice. Not all of us want to live alone, though, and some of us would find it difficult to live without the help and support of others. Still, living at home with parents may not seem like real adult living.

For learning disabled people whose learning disabilities and the problems of ADD make completely independent living a burden, but who want to live as adults independent of their parents, a different kind of setting may be a good solution. Group homes, in which several adults with learning disabilities share a home with an employed manager or managers, are becoming more and more common. In a group home, there is the opportunity for many kinds of shared experiences as well as the opportunity to have time alone.

Some group home clients share rooms; others may have their own rooms. Household chores, such as cooking, cleaning, and shopping, are usually shared, but clients have independent jobs and manage their own money, sometimes with the assistance of the manager or counselor.

Outings, parties, and holiday events may be shared, often including other family members, or group home clients may join their families for holidays. In many ways, group homes resemble the boarding houses of earlier days where single adults rented rooms in a home and took their meals together – except that the clients in group homes usually share more than just the living space and mealtime. Group homes vary. Some are very much like families, with residents sharing many outside activities as well as chores. Others are set up to be more independent, with only a few activities shared, and sometimes more of the household work done by hired workers. Of course, it is more expensive to live in a group setting where the household work must be paid for.

For another type of living arrangement, some special programs are available that assist adults with learning disabilities in making the transition from living at home to independent living in apartments. Frequently, assistance with locating an apartment, planning, management, and budgeting is available, with follow-up on a regular basis until the adult is able to manage with complete independence.

For information on these alternatives to traditional family living, the booklet *Resources for Adults with Learning Disabilities,* available from HEATH Resource Center, is a good source. The booklet is listed in the bibliography at the end of this book, and HEATH Resource Center's address is listed in the Resources section.

Special Issues

There are many issues about marriage and family life that we could discuss, but then this chapter might be far too long! It is not possible to cover all the problems that might arise just as it is not possible to present all the wonderful, happy things that might occur. Still, there are one or two special issues that need to be mentioned because of the particular relationship they have to learning disabilities.

It is important to state that these are not problems that are always associated with learning disabilities. That would be far from the truth. However, both of these serious problems, alcoholism and depression, seem to occur more frequently among people with learning disabilities than in the general population.

1. *Alcoholism and learning disabilities.* Alcoholism is a disease in which the individual's drinking of alcohol causes serious problems with relationships, health, money, employment, or a combination of these. While it is not curable, it is possible to control alcoholism through treatment and by refraining from consuming any alcoholic beverages at all. Because of the social and educational problems that people with learning disabilities experience, a greater risk for alcoholism may exist.

Many people with learning disabilities, especially those who also have Attention Deficit Disorder, have told me that they have found it harder to control their learning and behavioral problems when they drink, even if they drink very little. Those who have coordination problems often have found them much worse with even a small amount of alcohol in their systems. Others have found impulsivity harder to control.

Non-learning disabled people also find their ability to control their behavior diminished by the use of alcohol, of course, but the problem seems much greater for many of us with learning disabilities. Since many of us already must work very hard to cope with our learning disabilities, it may be a good idea to avoid drinking at all.

If you or someone you love drinks to such an extent that it is

202

interfering with family relationships, getting along with others, keeping or performing on the job, or if it is causing health or money problems, then the possibility of alcoholism should be considered. You may want to talk to your family doctor and contact Alcoholics Anonymous for assistance. If *you* are the problem drinker, Alcoholics Anonymous can help you help yourself. If someone you love has the problem, you can be referred to a support group that can help you deal with the problem in a way that is helpful to both of you.

2. *Depression and learning disabilities.* Depression is a condition in which a person is sad and emotionally withdrawn for a longer time and to a greater degree than his or her situation seems to suggest. Often, a depressed person feels so weighed down by troubles that he or she feels unable to function at all. A depressed person may sleep much more or much less than the average person and may have trouble doing the ordinary tasks of life. Depression is thought to be both an emotional and possibly a chemical disorder, and it often responds well to treatment. Some depressed people will have periods of time when they are doing very well and then will go into a period of depression.

Some experts feel that depression is more common among people with learning disabilities than in the normal population. Because those of us with learning disabilities are often frustrated by our disabilities and sometimes suffer poor self-concepts, our situations may be more likely to cause depression. Some theories of learning disabilities also seem to suggest some sort of biochemical lack of balance. This may also play a role in depression.

In the past, depressed people often got neither help nor sympathy. People did not understand that you couldn't just "snap out of it," which was what they would often say to depressed people. Now, however, people suffering from depression are often helped by medication. These drugs are given only by prescription, and a person taking them should follow the doctor's instructions carefully. No one should take more or less than prescribed without the doctor's consent and should never stop taking the medication without checking with the doctor first.

In a earlier chapter, I discussed the fact that some people with hyperactivity or Attention Deficit Disorder may take prescription drugs to help with their problems. Medication for depression is sometimes also given along with the drugs used for hyperactivity or ADD, and should be seen as one more possible way of helping control some of the problems caused by these conditions. I am not a medical doctor, so it is not my job to make decisions about medication. While I believe that we should not overuse drugs to solve our problems, I do feel strongly that there is much to be gained by discussing with your doctor the possibilities of using medications.

If you or someone you love has times of serious depression, contact your family doctor. He or she can refer you to a specialist who can help.

Summary

In this chapter, we have looked at some of the special problems in marriage and family life that may be affected by learning disabilities. Our focus has been on looking for ways to make those alternatives to traditional family roles and settings. Throughout the chapter, honest and open communication with other people in your family has been stressed. The more honestly you are able to share your feeling, beliefs, strengths, and weaknesses with the people you love and who love you, the better you will know yourself and the others in your family, and the more easily you can work together to make your life fulfilling and successful.

Glossary

This glossary includes, in simple language, definitions for many of the terms used in this book. These definitions may not be the same as those used by others, but the words are defined according to the way I have used them in this book. Some of the terms have general meanings as well as specific meanings that relate to the field of learning disabilities, but only the definitions needed to understand the usage here have been given. Of course, when considering educational or legal eligibility, more technical or legal definitions would be used.

ACT: American College Test, a standardized test used by many colleges and universities as one of the requirements for admission. The test may be taken with special accommodations for students with learning disabilities.

ADD: the abbreviation for Attention Deficit Disorder (see below).

ADHD: the abbreviation for Attention Deficit Hyperactivity Disorder (see below).

acceptance: a stage in coming to terms with a disability in which one recognizes both personal limitations and personal strengths and begins to move on with one's life.

accessibility: degree to which handicapped individuals are able to use a service or program. For example, if a high score on a reading test is a requirement for a job, the job may not be accessible to a person with a reading disability.

accommodations: changes or alterations in the ways something is done so that a handicapped person is able to have equal access. For example, accommodations for a learning disabled college student may include more time to take a test, or a notetaker to attend class and take notes for the student's use. Job accommodations may include giving oral instructions to a worker who does not read.

achievement test: a test designed to measure the level a person has reached in specific school-related skills as compared to other persons. The tests are divided into sections related to particular skills, and the scores usually indicate a grade level that the person has achieved in that skill.

alcoholism: a disease in which the individual's drinking of alcohol causes serious problems with relationships, health, money, or employment, or a combination of these. While it is not curable, it is possible to control alcoholism through treatment and refraining from consuming any alcoholic beverages.

allergen: a substance that causes an allergic reaction in a person who is sensitive to it. For example, pollen may be an allergen which makes a person sneeze when exposed to it.

allergy: a sensitivity to certain substances in the environment that causes a reaction, such as sneezing, rash, mood problems, stomach upset, etc. There are many kinds of allergic reactions, including some behavioral and learning difficulties. Some experts feel allergies may be a cause of some kinds of learning disabilities.

alternative testing: administration of the same test as that given to other students, but under different conditions. For example, a learning disabled student may take the test in another location in order to be free from distraction or noise, may have the test read aloud, or may take an oral test.

206

ameliorate: to make a condition less damaging, even if it cannot be eliminated. For example, if a person uses notes as reminders, she may be said to have *ameliorated* her memory problems.

Americans with Disabilities Act: a law guaranteeing disabled individuals access to jobs and public places, including requirements that accommodations be made for disabled individuals in various kinds of work places.

assessment: an evaluation of an individual's abilities and disabilities, based on testing and observation by one or more trained persons.

Attention Deficit Disorder: a condition in which a person has problems in abilities related to directing or maintaining his or her attention to the normal tasks of learning and functioning. The abbreviation *ADD* is often used. See *Attention Deficit Hyperactivity Disorder* (ADHD) for more information, and *Strauss syndrome* for information on a previously used, related term.

Attention Deficit Hyperactivity Disorder: a newer name for the condition known as Attention Deficit Disorder. The abbreviation is *ADHD*. Generally, the primary problem areas are considered to be attention problems and impulsivity. Some experts consider hyperactivity to be an important component of this disorder, as the name implies. Others disagree and may continue to use the earlier term, *Attention Deficit Disorder,* and suggest that it be specified as being with or without hyperactivity.

auditory: having to do with hearing. For example, auditory ability is the ability to hear.

auditory learner: a person who learns better by hearing than by vision.

auditory acuity: level at which someone is able to hear. This does not necessarily relate to how well the person learns through hearing, just how well or how badly his or her ears and nerves of hearing receive and transmit sound to the brain. For example, a person with good auditory acuity hears well; one with poor auditory acuity may need a hearing aid.

auditory discrimination: ability to tell differences and similarities in what is heard. For example, a person who has trouble discriminating between "Perry" or "Barry" when introduced to someone may have poor auditory discrimination.

auditory memory: ability to recall information taken in through hearing. For example, a person who remembers what is heard very well is said to have good auditory memory.

Better Business Bureau: organization of business people in a community involved in dealing with complaints about business. While they cannot recommend one firm over another, they can inform consumers if a certain business has a number of unsatisfied complaints against it.

body image: mental view a person has of his or her body. For example, a person who does not have a good idea of how much space his or her body takes up may not know whether there is room to join friends sitting on a bench or may not have a feeling of whether he or she is standing up straight.

body language: information conveyed to others by the position of the body. For example, one who turns away with arms crossed may convey a message of disinterest in hearing what is being said.

catastrophic reaction: overreaction to minor situations or happenings. For example, a person may become so angry and upset when a pencil breaks that he or she throws it across the room and cannot complete a simple task.

civil rights: rights guaranteed to a person by the constitution and laws of the United States.

Civil Rights Commission: agency charged with ensuring that individuals' civil rights are not violated. For example, persons who believe that they have been denied a job because of a learning disability might contact the local office of the Civil Rights Commission for advice and assistance.

circumvent: to work around a problem. For example, using taped books to complete a reading assignment for an English class is a way to circumvent a serious reading problem.

chemical imbalance: a medical problem in which certain substances the body needs are not present in the right amounts. For example, a person with some kinds of chemical imbalance may have more memory problems than normal.

college: generally, a four-year institution of higher learning. the term is also used to refer to any institution of higher education. See also *community college, junior college,* and *university* below.

community college: a two-year institution of higher education, located in a community and supported by it. The programs may include courses in technical training or those needed to complete the freshman and sophomore years towards a bachelor's degree. (see also *junior college.*)

counselor: a member of the helping professions who works with individuals or groups in learning ways to deal with problems. The term is sometimes used generally for a variety of helping professionals, such as psychologists and therapists, but is also often used as a term for those with specific training in one of several fields. For example, the term *licensed professional counselor* indicates that the person has passed specific requirements for counseling work.

cursive: the general name for the handwriting style in which the letters are joined. It is usually taught in late second grade or early third grade although some experts recommend using it for children with learning disabilities from the beginning of school.

denial: refusing to accept a condition or situation. For example, a person in the denial stage of adjusting to a disability may be unable to accept that there are certain things that he or she will be unable to do.

depression: a condition in which a person is sad and emotionally withdrawn for a longer time and to a greater degree than his or her situation seems to suggest.

developmental dyslexia: one of the names for learning disability. Originally, *developmental dyslexia* meant primarily a very serious reading problem in children. The word *developmental* was used to point out that this condition was not necessarily the same as *acquired dyslexia* or *alexia*, a very serious reading problem which a person might have following a head injury, or after some other injury to the brain.

diagnosis: a determination of what a person's condition is, including information on possible causes, degree of the condition, what treatment is recommended, and how the condition might be expected to change with treatment. Most people use the term *diagnosis* just to refer to the name of a particular condition, but a full diagnosis includes much more information.

diagnosis-shopping: a part of the denial stage of adjusting to a disability in which the person (or, in the case of a child, the parents) go from one doctor or clinic to another, hoping that someone will either say there is no problem, or that the problem is something less serious.

disability: a condition in which a person has less than normal ability in some function. For example, a person may have a reading disability in that he or she is unable to read at all. Many people use the terms *disability* and *handicap* as though they were the same. Some people, though, use the word *disability* to refer to the actual condition itself and *handicap* to refer to the amount of overall limitation the disability places upon the person in his or her particular situation. For example, a person with a reading disability may not have a handicap if his or her situation does not require much reading, and ways are developed to work around the problem when it does.

distractibility: a condition in which a person's attention is easily drawn away from what he or she is doing. For example, one who is visually distractible may find that he or she keeps looking away from the book in a room that is full of activity. An auditorially distractible person may find that any noise pulls attention away from the task.

dysgraphia: a severe problem in writing. Sometimes the term is used to refer both to severe problems in actually forming the letters and words on the page and to written expression, but more often, it refers to a disability in getting ideas expressed in writing. The term *dysorthographia* (see below) is a related term.

dyslexia: one of the most controversial terms used to mean a variety of things to different people. Some use it to mean only a very severe reading disability. It is now more commonly used to refer to learning disabilities in general. (See the definition for *learning disability* below.) Generally, *dyslexia* refer to problems that a person has probably always had. When it is a problem that shows up in a person whose ability was normal before an accident or illness involving the brain, it is called *alexia.*

dysorthographia: a severe problem in forming words and letters on paper. (See *dysgraphia* above.)

dyspedagogia: a term some experts have used to describe problems in learning which may be caused by poor or inexperienced teaching.

emotional disturbance: severe, fairly long-term problems with feelings, emotions, learning, or relationships when compared with other persons of similar age, ability, or situation. Emotional disturbance is not considered a cause of learning disability as the term is normally used because learning problems caused by emotional disturbance most often are eliminated when and if the person's emotional problems are improved.

emotional lability: having mood swings. For example, a person with emotional lability may be quite happy one minute and upset the next minute without any noticeable cause.

figure-ground discrimination problem: a perceptual problem in which the person is unable to pick out the important information from the background. For example, the person with visual figure-ground problems may have trouble picking out the words printed on an advertisement that uses a photograph of scenery as the background. An auditory figure-ground problem may make it hard for a person to follow a conversation when there is music playing.

GED: General Education Diploma, or General Educational Development test, commonly called a high-school equivalency diploma. Passing the test indicates that the person has acquired the knowledge required for a high school education, even if he or she has not graduated formally from high school.

genetic counselor: a person who assists individuals or families in examining their family backgrounds to see if certain kinds of inherited conditions are present.

group home: a home in which several adults with disabilities share a house with an employed manager or counselor. Often there are many social activities arranged. In some group homes, a person may share a room or may room alone. Cooking, cleaning, shopping, yard work, and other chores are usually shared, but clients have independent jobs and manage their own money, sometimes with the assistance of the manager or counselor.

handicap: a condition in which a person has a disability which causes less than normal function in certain life activities. For example, persons with severe reading disabilities may have handicaps if they are in a job or social situations where reading is important and they have not found ways to acquire the information in ways other than reading.

higher learning: a term which usually refers to education after high school. (See also post-secondary education below.)

hyperactivity: excessive activity when compared with others of the same age and in similar situations.

impulsivity: acting or speaking without considering the consequences or taking into account other factors. For example, a person with impulsivity may see an old friend and say, "Gee, you've put on weight!" without thinking that the remark may have hurt the person's feelings. Or a person may turn or move suddenly while standing in line without thinking that the person directly behind may be stepped on or jostled.

inner ear difficulties: problems with the part of the ear which controls the nerves of hearing and balance. Some experts have suggested that the balance portion of the inner ear may be involved in some learning disabilities.

input: information that is taken in through one or more of the senses. For example, *visual input* is information a person receives through seeing it.

invisible handicap: a condition that limits one's ability to function, but which cannot be seen. For example, an individual using a wheelchair has a visible handicap, but the handicap of a person with learning disabilities cannot be seen.

junior college: an older term used to refer to a community college (see above). The term is becoming less common because it suggested that these institutions were of less stature than four-year colleges rather than intended for different but related purposes.

LD: the abbreviation for learning disability.

L/LD: the abbreviation for *language/learning disability* (see below), one of the terms used for learning disability.

214

language/learning disability: a term used in some states to refer to learning disability. It suggests the belief that learning disabilities are related to an inability in using language in one or more of its forms, such as reading, writing, speaking, or even in mental processes involving the language of arithmetic and mathematics.

learning center: a place in a college or university where students may go for assistance with learning skills, tutoring, alternative testing forms, etc. In some cases, the centers are open to all students; in others, they are especially designed for learning disabled students.

learning disability: the most common term used to refer to a permanent condition in which an individual with otherwise good overall ability has difficulty in learning and using certain kinds of information, or in learning in particular ways. While the cause may not be known, it is *not* low intelligence, emotional disorders, poor teaching or lack of educational opportunity, or sensory loss, such as poor vision or hearing. Some physical, attentional, or behavioral characteristics may or may not accompany and complicate the learning disability, such as hyperactivity, distractibility, poor coordination, impulsiveness, and others, but these are not the cause.

light load: fewer than the average number of courses usually taken by a college student. This is an accommodation which might be selected by a student with a learning disability who needs more study time, or more time to listen to books on tape.

literalness: a tendency to interpret things exactly as said rather than according to common usage. For example, a person with this problem who hears someone say, "Debbie uses flowery language" may think Debbie talks about flowers rather than understanding that what is meant is that Debbie uses very fancy, elaborate expressions.

manuscript: the form of writing often called *printing*. It is normally the style used in first and second grades. The letters are generally vertical with separate strokes for each part of the letter, although some new styles are now being used more frequently in which there is a slant to the letters, letters are made with some retracing so that there are fewer strokes, and final strokes are used so that the change to cursive (see above) is easier.

mental retardation: serious learning, social, and adaptive problems resulting from a permanent lowering of an individual's intelligence and ability to function. The condition occurred very early, before birth or shortly after. Although a person with mental retardation has difficulty in learning, the learning problems are more general than those of people with learning disability. Mental retardation and learning disability are not at all the same condition.

mirror writing: a problem in writing in which the person writes backwards, from left to right, so that the words appear as they would in a mirror. Usually, mirror writing is seen in only part of a person's written work. With some learning disabled children and adults, it may appear to be set off when writing on the back of thin paper when the reversed material on the other side can be seen, or in young children, when writing material that starts closer to the right hand side of the page, such as a second column of words.

modality: a way in which a person learns or receives information. For example, the visual modality refers to taking in information through the eyes. Learning in the visual modality would be recommended for someone who tended to be able to take in information better through the eyes. In the past, one of the methods suggested for helping children with learning disabilities was *modality training,* in which attempts were made to improve ability in a weak modality. In general, the approach was not as successful as the experts had hoped.

negotiation: a stage in adjusting to a disability in which a person mentally bargains with himself or higher powers about the condition: "I'll never be bad again if this just isn't so" or, in later stages of acceptance, "I can't achieve this goal, so I'll try for another one."

neurological: relating to the nerves or the brain.

neurological disorder: a disorder caused by damage or disease of the brain or nervous system. For example, because learning disability was thought to be caused by brain damage, this term has often been used.

notetaker: an individual, usually paid, who attends class with a learning disabled student to take notes for that student.

output: information given by a person. For example, to respond to directions from a teacher, a student may give verbal output by speaking, or written output by writing or typing.

overactivity: more than normal activity for a person of a particular age or situation. (See *hyperactivity* above.)

PL 93-112: see Public Law 93-112 below.

PL 94-142: see Public Law 94-142 below.

perceptual disorder: a disorder in interpreting information received through the senses. For example, one may have very good vision, yet may have problems in making sense out of what one sees, so that although the eyes take in the word *was,* the brain cannot tell whether the word is *was* or *saw.* Or a person may have figure-ground discrimination problems (see above), or any of several kinds of difficulties in which the senses get the information but the brain cannot interpret it well.

penmanship: an older term used to refer to the skill of handwriting. Practice in penmanship has less emphasis in school today.

peripheral vision: sight at the extreme outside edges of one's field of sight.

perseveration: continuing to do something longer than appropriate. For example, persons with perseveration may erase so long that he or she wears a hole in the paper, or pick at a snag in an article of clothing until it is much worse. A person with verbal perseveration may chatter on and on inappropriately.

personal space: the amount of space around a person that the person considers as belonging to him or her. The amount varies, depending on such factors as the relationship with another person. For example, a person usually is comfortable with less personal space in an interaction with a close friend than with a stranger or someone known only through business contacts. Many people with learning disabilities have trouble being aware of the personal space of other people.

post-secondary education: education or training after high school. Post-secondary education may refer to college or university work, or to technical or vocational training programs.

prognosis: the expected outcome of a condition. For example, if a person with learning disability receives help and support early, the *prognosis* may be very good.

psychiatrist: a medical doctor who specializes in working with people with emotional and mental disorders, and who has had specialized training in the field.

psychologist: a person with training in psychology who works with people with emotional and behavioral disorders, or who may work in a number of other areas, such as research in learning, or in assessment of mental abilities. Usually, a psychologist has a PhD degree, although in some places, a person may be a school psychologist (see below) without this degree.

Public Law 93-112: the Rehabilitation Act of 1973, guaranteeing certain rights of access to employment and other services from agencies that receive federal funding. (See Section 504 below).

Public Law 94-142: the Education for All Handicapped Children Act of 1975. This law required that all handicapped children be given an appropriate education at no cost to the parents in the setting that would be least restrictive to their overall development.

reauditorization: saying silently to one's self something that he or she has heard before. For example, an auditory learner may spell a word silently before writing it

Ritalin: one of the drugs used by prescription for treatment of hyperactivity.

SAT: Scholastic Aptitude Test, a standardized test used by many colleges and universities as one of the requirements for admission. The test may be taken with special accommodations for students with learning disabilities.

scribe: a person who writes for a learning disabled person, exactly as the learning disabled person dictates, either during a test or the completion of an assignment.

Section 504: a part of the Rehabilitation Act of 1973, or Public Law 93-112. This law states that handicapped individuals have rights to employment and a variety of other services from any public or private agency which receives federal financial assistance.

sensory loss: usually refers to lessening of ability in hearing or vision, although it may also refer to a loss of ability to gain information through touch.

short attention span: inability to pay attention to something for a long period of time compared to others of the same age. For example, a person with a short attention span may be able to watch a half-hour television show, but not a two-hour special. For some children with learning disabilities or Attention Deficit Disorder, the attention span may be only a few minutes.

slow learner syndrome: a term originally used to refer to individuals whose intelligence was somewhat below normal, but not low enough to be considered mentally retarded. For a time, the term was unfortunately used for learning disabilities as well, even though people whose primary problem is learning disability have intelligence that is normal or above. The term is now used again as it was originally, to refer to people below normal but not mentally retarded who may need some special assistance in learning and social adjustment. For example, a person who is a slow learner may function in school and socially on the level of a slightly younger person.

social imperception: difficulty in interpreting social situations through inability to interpret facial expression, tone of voice, body language, or other cues. For example, a person with social imperception may not understand that a host's yawning and looking at his watch may mean that it is time to go home.

social worker: a person in the helping professions who specializes in assisting individuals or families in social or life situations. Social workers may have different levels of training, depending on the job requirements, ranging from bachelor's degrees through doctorates. Some, such as psychiatric social workers, will have had considerable advanced training.

specific learning disability: one of the early terms for learning disability that emphasizes the fact that the condition is not one of overall lowered ability but is in one or more specific areas. For example, a student with specific learning disability may excel in mathematics but do poorly in language arts subjects.

spell checker: a system built into a computer, word processor, or typewriter that checks each word to see if it is actually a word. The system can catch most spelling errors and many typographical errors, but it cannot catch errors in which the word typed is actually a word. For example, if the writer types *writting* instead of *writing,* the system will signal that it is an error, but if the writer types *righting* instead of *writing,* it will not.

stimulus-bound: being so caught up with one thing that

attention is not easily changed. For example, a person who is stimulus-bound may not hear his or her name being called when looking at a textbook.

Strauss syndrome: an older term which generally describes what is now called Attention Deficit Hyperactivity Disorder. It was named for Dr. Alfred Strauss, who originally thought that the condition was caused by brain damage. He based his ideas on his observations of similar behaviors in young war veterans who were normal learners before receiving brain injuries in battle. Although experts in the field of learning disabilities criticized his ideas for a while, recognition of the fact that his work was important in suggesting that problems in learning were not always caused by mental retardation led many to use his name to refer to the condition.

The term *Strauss syndrome* is used to describe the condition of a person who has a number of the following symptoms, though not necessarily all of them (see also each of the symptoms alphabetically in this glossary):

distractibility

perseveration

short attention span

impulsivity

hyperactivity

figure-ground discrimination problems

memory problems

learning problems

emotional lability

catastrophic reaction

support group: a group of individuals who meet to assist each other in coping with problems related to a specific situation or condition. Usually, there is no professional leader directing the group, although some may assist. The members meet mostly socially to help one another. For example, a learning disabilities support group in a college setting may get together for brown-bag lunches just to discuss their problems and successes and to give each other suggestions on study strategies.

syndrome: a condition that includes a number, but not necessarily all, of a group of symptoms identified by experts. For example, one person with Strauss syndrome may be hyperactive, distractible, impulsive, and have learning problems, but not have figure-ground perception problems, while another with the same syndrome may have all of the same problems except hyperactivity.

tactile defensiveness: a problem in responding normally to touch. For example, a person may jump when touched lightly even knowing in advance that touching will occur. Or a person may be very uncomfortable just being touched. Some may prefer a firm touch or grip; others may not like to be touched at all.

tactile-kinesthetic: relating to the sense of touch and the feeling of movement, or, more simply, touching and doing. For example, the tactile-kinesthetic modality is being used when a person practices spelling by writing the words over and over.

technology: use of modern devices to make work easier or faster. For example, a spell checker on a typewriter is an example of technology that is helpful to many people with learning disabilities.

therapist: a person engaged in a specific form of treatment. Very often, the term *therapist* when used alone has no legal definition. Some types of therapists, such as speech therapists, occupational therapists, or physical therapists, have very extensive training and high professional requirements. Other types of therapists, such as some reading therapists or learning therapists, may have training only in one specific method.

university: an institution of higher learning including four-year degrees and advanced work, such as master's and doctoral degrees. A university may contain several colleges, such as a college of education, college of engineering, etc.

visual: referring to what is seen. For example, visual ability is the ability to see.

visual discrimination: ability to see similarities and differences. For example, a person with poor visual discrimination may have trouble telling a square from a rectangle, or seeing the differences between a capital *I*, a lower-case *l*, and a numeral *1*.

visualization: making mental pictures of things or actions. For example, a visual learner may make a mental picture of the three things he or she wants to pick up at the store to help remember them.

visual learner: a person who learns better when information is received through the eyes.

visual memory: ability to remember what is seen. For example, persons with good visual memory remember very well what they see.

Vocational Rehabilitation: state and federal agency

concerned with assisting people with disabilities to become functioning workers. Persons who qualify may receive funds for education or training to help them get appropriate jobs.

vocational school: a school that provides training for a specific kind of job. Many are private, profit making concerns. Quality and cost vary greatly.

Resources

College Entrance Testing

ACT Test Administration
Universal special Testing - 61
P.O. Box 4028
Iowa City, IA 52243
(319) 337-1332

Admissions Testing Program
ATP Services for Handicapped Students
P.O. Box 6226
Princeton, NJ 08541-6226
(609) 921-9000

Organizations

Disability Rights and Education Fund, Inc.
2212 6th Street
Berkeley, CA 94710
(415) 644-2555

Association on Higher Education And Disability (AHEAD)
   (formerly Association on Handicapped Student Service
   Programs in Postsecondary Education [AHSSPPE])
P.O. Box 21192
Columbus, OH 43221-0192
(614) 488-4972

Attention Deficit Disorder Association
P.O. Box 488
West Newbury, MA 01985

Council for Exceptional Children
Division for Learning Disabilities
1920 Association Drive
Reston, VA 22091-1589
Council on Learning Disabilities
P.O. Box 40303
Overland Park, KS 66204

National Center for Children with Learning Disabilities
99 Park Avenue
New York, NY 10016
(212) 687-7211

Learning Disabilities Association of America (formerly
    Association for Children and Adults with Learning
    Disabilities)
4156 Library Road
Pittsburgh, PA 15234
(412) 341-1515

Orton Dyslexia Society
Chester Building, Suite 382
Baltimore, MD 21204-6020
(800) 222-3123

President's Committee on Employment of Citizens with
    Disabilities
1331 F. Street, NW
Washington, DC 20004-1107
(202) 376-6200 (voice)
(202) 376-6205 (TDD)

Self-Help Groups

ADDult Support Network
c/o Mary Jane Johnson
2620 Ivy Place
Toledo, OH 43613

Marin Puzzle People
17 Buena Vista Avenue
Mill Valley, CA 94941
(415) 383-8763

National Network of Learning Disabled Adults (NNLDA)
808 West 82nd Street, F-2
Scottsdale, AZ 85257
The Network is an organization of learning disabled individuals
and representatives of a number of support organizations for
learning disabled adults. A newsletter, the *National Networker,*
available through editor Bill Butler, (602) 941-5112 at a very low
cost, includes news, resources, general information, and tips.

Information Agencies

HEATH Resource Center
(Higher Education and the Handicapped)
1 Dupont Circle, Suite 789
Washington, DC 20036-1193
(800) 544-3284

National Information Center for Children and Youth with
Disabilities
P.O. Box 1492
Washington, DC 20013-1492
(800) 999-5599

Recorded Books for Print Handicapped and Blind

National Library Service for the Blind and Physically
    Handicapped
Library of Congress
1291 Taylor Street N.W.
Washington, DC 20542
(800) 424-8567

Recording for the Blind
20 Roszel Road
Princeton, NJ 08540
(609) 452-0606

Bibliography

Books

Aslett, D. (1991). *Not for packrats only.* New York: Penguin.

Barr, A., Donahue, W., Podrid, A., Seelig, S., Capute, E., Holloway, S., Rubin, C., & Weinger, L. (1987). *Successful college tutoring: Focusing on the learning disabled student in the learning center.* Long island, NY: Long Island University.

Butzberger, K.L. (1992). *A literature review and recommendations: Alcoholism and learning disabled students.* Unpublished master's professional paper, Texas Woman's University, Denton.

Chesler, B. (1990). *A talking mouth speaks: About learning disabled college students.* Sacramento, CA: Author.

Clark, G.M., & Kolstoe, O.P. (1990). *Career development and transition for adolescents with disabilities.* Boston: Allyn & Bacon.

Cordoni, B. (1990). *Living with a learning disability* (rev. ed.). Carbondale, IL: Southern Illinois University.

Cruickshank, W.R., Morse, W.C., & Johns, J. (1980). *Learning disabilities: The struggle from adolescence toward adulthood.* Syracuse, NY: Syracuse University.

East, J. (1987). *Yes you can! A booklet to help young people with learning disabilities understand and help themselves* (rev. ed.). Chicage: National Easter Seal Society.

Galvin, M. (1988). *Otto learns about his medicine: A story about medication for hyperactive children.* New York: Magination (Brunner/Mazel).

Garnett, K., & Gerber, P. (1985). *Life transitions of learning disabled adults: Perspectives from several countries.* New York: World Rehabilitation Fund.

Garnett, K., & LaPorta, S. (1984). *Dispelling the myths: College students and learning disabilities.* New York: Hunter College.

Gilson, J. (1980). *Do bananas chew gum?.* New York: Lothrop, Lee & Shepard.

Greenberg, G.S., & Horn, W.F. (1991). *Attention deficit hyperactivity disorder: Questions and answers for parents.* Champaign, IL: Research Press.

Griggs, M.J., & Wiar, C.M. (1986). *Living with a learning disability: A handbook for high school and college students.* Waterford, MI: Minerva.

Hayes, M.L. (1974). *The tuned-in, turned on book about learning problems.* Novato, CA: Academic Therapy.

Hedrick, L.H. (1990). *Five days to an organized life.* New York: Dell.

Johnson, D.J., & Blalock, J.W. (Eds.). (1987). *Adults with learning disabilities.* Orlando, FL: Grune & Stratton.

Lasker, J. (1974). *He's my brother.* Chicago: Albert Whitman.

Learning Disabilities Association of Canada. (undated). *Job interview tips for people with learning disabilities.* Ottowa, Ontario, Canada: Author.

Lerner, J. (1992). *Learning disabilities: Theories, diagnosis, and teaching strategies* (6th ed.). Boston: Houghton Mifflin.

Scheiber, B., & Talpers, J. (1987). *Unlocking potential: College and other choices for learning disabled people: A step-by-step guide.* Bethesda, MD: Adler & Adler.

Schwarz, J. (1992). *Another door to learning: True stories of learning disabled children & adults, and the keys to their success.* New York: Crossroad.

Simpson, E. (1979. *Reversals: A personal account of victory over dyslexia.* Boston: Houghton Mifflin.

Smith, B.K. (1981). *Inside out or outside in? Perceptions of the learning-disabled young person.* Austin, TX: Hogg Foundation.

Smith, S.L. (1980). *No easy answers: The learning disabled child at home and at school.* New York: Bantam.

Smith, S.L. (1991). *Succeeding against the odds: Strategies and insights from the learning disabled.* Los Angeles, CA: Jeremy P. Tarcher.

U.S. Department of Justice, Civil Rights Division (undated). *The Americans with Disabilities Act: Questions and answers.* Washington, DC: Author.

Vogel, S.A. (1990). *College students with learning disabilities: A handbook* (3rd Ed.). Pittsburgh, PA: ACLD Bookstore.

Wolverton, C. (1992). *Assisting learning disabled students in evaluating college programs.* Unpublished master's professional paper, Texas Woman's University, Denton.

Woods, J.E. (1989). *How to succeed in college with dyslexia.* Dallas, TX: Sem-Co.

Wren, C.,Adelman, P., Pike, M.B., & Wilson, J.L. (1987). *College and the high school student with learning disabilities: The student's perspective.* Chicago, IL: DePaul University.

Wren, C., & Segal, L. (1991). *College students with learning disabilities: A student's perspective* (2nd Ed.). Chicago, IL: DePaul University.

Guides

Jarrow, J., Baker, B., Hartman, R., Harris, R., Lesh, K., Redden, M., & Smithson, J. (1986). *How to choose a college: Guide for the student with a disability.* Columbus, OH: Association of Handicapped Student Service Programs in Postsecondary Education (AHSSPPE) and Higher Education and the Handicapped (HEATH).

Liscio, M.A. (1984). *A guide to colleges for learning disabled students.* Orlando, FL: Academic Press.

Mangrum, C.T., II, & Strichart, S.S. (1984). *College and the learning disabled student: A guide to program selection, development, and implementation.* Orlando, FL: Grune & Stratton.

Mangrum, C.T., II, & Strichart, S.S. (1988). *Peterson's colleges with programs for learning-disabled students* (2nd Ed.). Princeton, NJ: Peterson's Guides.

Scheiber, B., & Talpers, J. (1985). *Campus access for learning disabled students: A comprehensive guide.* Washington, DC: Closer Look.

Scheiber, B., & Talpers, J. (1987). *Unlocking potential: College and other choices for learning disabled people: A step-by-step guide.* Bethesda, MD: Adler & Adler.

Slovak, I. (1984). *BOSC directory of facilities for learning disabled people.* Congers, NY: BOSC.

Smith, L.M. (1980). *The college student with a disability: A faculty handbook.* Washington, DC: President's Committee on the Employment of People with Disabilities (formerly President's Committee on the Employment of the Handicapped).

Straughn, C.T., & Colby, S.C. (1985). *Lovejoy's college guide for the learning disabled.* New York: Monarch

Sullivan, C. (1985). *Teaching learning disabled students in college.* Northern Virginia Community College: Author.

Thomas, C.H., & Thomas, J.L. (1986). *Directory of college facilities and services for the disabled* (2nd ed.). Phoenix, AZ: Oryx.

Vogel, S.A. (1990). *College students with learning disabilities: A handbook* (3rd ed.). Pittsburgh, PA: LDA Bookstore.

Wilson, L. (Ed.). (1982). *New directions for college learning assistance: Helping special students.* San Francisco: Jossey-Bass.

Woods, J.E. (1989). *How to succeed in college with dyslexia.* Dallas, TX: Sem-Co.

Articles

Abrams, H.G., & Abrams, R.H. (1981). Legal obligations toward the post-secondary learning disabled student. *Wayne Law Review, 27,* 1475-1499.

Aksamit, D., Morris, M., & Leuenberger, J. (1987). Preparation of student services professionals and faculty for serving learning disabled college students. *Journal of College Student Personnel, 12,* 53-59.

Alfred, R.L., & Lum, G.D. (1988). Remedial program policies, student demographic characteristics, and academic achievement in community colleges. *Community/Junior College Quarterly, 12,* 107-120.

Barbaro, F. (1982). The learning disabled college student: Some considerations in setting objectives. *Journal of Learning Disabilities, 15,* 599-603.

Barbaro, F., Christman, D., Holzinger, S.M., & Rosenburg, E. (1985). Support services for the learning disabled college student. *Social Work, 30,* 12-18.

Birely, M., & Manley, E. (1980). The learning disabled college student in a college environment: A report of Wright State University's program. *Journal of Learning Disabilities, 13,* 12-15.

Blackburn, J.C., & Locacchini, E.V. (1981). Student service responsibilities of institutions to learning disabled students. *College and University, 57,* 208-217.

Blalock, G. & Dixon, N. (1982). Improving prospects for the college-bound learning disabled. *Topics in Learning and Learning Disabilities, 2,* 69-78.

Brill, J. (1987). Learning disabled adults in postsecondary education. Washington, DC: American Council on Education.

Buchanan, M., & Wolf, J.S. (1986). A comprehensive study of learning disabled adults. *Journal of Learning Disabilities, 19,* 34-38,

Bursuck, W.D., Rose, E., Cowen, S., & Yahaya, M.A. (1989). Nationwide survey of postsecondary education services for students with learning disabilities. *Exceptional Children, 56,* 236-245.

Collinson, M. N.-K. (1989, March 8). At college Misericordia, learning disabled students discover ways to work around their handicaps. *Chronicle of Higher Education,* 29-30.

Cooper, R.J. (1987). What an admission counselor needs to know about learning disabled students. *Journal of College Admissions, 116,* 14-19.

Cordoni, B. (1979). Assisting dyslexic college students: An experimental program design at a university. *Bulletin of the Orton Society, 29,* 263-268.

Cordoni, B. (1982). A directory of college LD services. *Journal of Learning Disabilities, 15,* 529-533.

Cordoni, B.K. (1982). Post-secondary education: Where do we go from here? *Journal of Learning Disabilities, 15,* 265-267.

Cronin, M.E., & Gerber, P.J., (1982). Preparing the learning disabled adolescent for adulthood. *Topics in Learning and Learning Disabilities, 2*(3), 55-68.

Cowen, S. (1985). College choice for the learning disabled. *Academic Therapy, 21,* 77-82.

Dalke, C., & Schmidt, S. (1987). Meeting the transitional needs of college-bound students with learning disabilities. *Journal of learning disabilities, 20,* 176-180.

Decker, T.W., Polloway, E.A., & Decker, B.B. (1985). Help for the LD college student. *Academic Therapy, 20,* 339-345.

Deshler, D.D., Schumaker, J.B., Alley, G.R., Warner, M.M., & Clark, F.L. (1982). Learning disabilities in adolescent and young adult populations: Research implications. *Focus on Exceptional Children, 15*(1), 1-12.

Dexter, B. (1982). Helping learning disabled students prepare for college. *Journal of Learning Disabilities, 15,* 344-346.

Engel, J.B. (1988). Questions to ask the bright but learning disabled student during the admissions process. *College and University, 63*(4), 333-337.

Hoffman, J., Sheldon, K.L., Minskoff, E.H., Sautter, S.W., Steidle, E.F., Baker, P.D., Bailey, M.B., & Echols, L.D. (1987). Needs of learning disabled adults. *Journal of Learning Disabilities, 20,* 43-52.

Hoy, C. (1986). Learning disabled students. *Journal of College Admissions, 112:* 10-14.

Johnston, C.L. (1984). The learning disabled adolescent and young adult: An overview and critique of current practice. *Journal of Learning Disabilities, 17,* 386-391.

Kahn, M.S. (1980). Learning problems of the secondary and junior college learning disabled student: Suggested remedies. *Journal of Learning Disabilities. 13,* 40-44.

Keeney, L., & Smith, N. (1984). Foreign language modifications for disabled students: The campus response. *AHSSPPE Bulletin, 2*(1), 4-5.

Knowles, B.S., & Knowles, P.S. (1983). A model for identifying learning disabilities in college-bound students. *Journal of Learning Disabilities, 16,* 39-42.

Levine, S., & Osbourne, S. (1989, April). Living and learning with dyslexia. *Phi Delta Kappan, 70,* 594-598.

Lieberman, L.M. (1986). Is the learning disabled adult really necessary? *Journal of Learning Disabilities, 19,* 64.

Lundeberg, M., & Svien, K. (1988). Developing faculty understanding of college students with learning disabilities. *Journal of Learning Disabilities, 21,* 299-300, 306.

Matthews, P.R. (1987). Faculty attitudes toward accommodations for college students with learning disabilities. *Learning Disabilities Focus, 3,* 46-52.

McGuire, J.M., & O'Donnell, J.M. (1987). Helping learning disabled students to achieve: Collaboration between the faculty and support services. *College Teaching, 37,* 29-32.

Putnam, M.L. (1984). Post-secondary education for learning disabled students: A review of the literature. *Journal of College Student Personnel, 25,* 68-75.

Rosenthal, I. (1986). New directions for service delivery to learning disabled youth and young adults. *Learning Disabilities Focus, 2*(1), 55-61.

Ryan, A.G., & Heikkila, M.K. (1988). Learning disabilities in higher education: Misconceptions. *Academic Therapy, 24,* 177-190.

Sachs, J.J., Iliff, V.W., & Donnelly, R.F. (1987). Oh, OK, I'm LD! *Journal of Learning Disabilities, 20,* 92-93.

Salend, S.J., Salend, S.M., & Yanok, J. (1985). Learning disabled students in higher education: The role of the special education faculty. *Teacher Education and Special Education, 8,* 48-54.

Saracoglu, B., Minden, H., & Wilchesky, M. (1989). The adjustment of students with learning disabilities to university and its relationship to self-esteem and self-efficacy. *Journal of Learning Disabilities, 22,* 590-592.

Vogel, S.A. (1981). On developing college LD Programs. *Journal of Learning Disabilities, 15,* 518-528.

White, W.J., Alley, G.R., Deshler, D.D., Schumaker, J.B., Warner, M.M., & Clark, F.L. (1982). Are there learning disabilities after high school? *Exceptional Children, 49,* 273-274.

Wiseman, R.L., Emry, R.A., & Morgan, D. (1988). Predicting academic success for disabled students in higher education. *Research in Higher Education, 28,* 255-269.

Yanok, J. (1985). Modifying academic requirements for learning disabled students enrolled in teacher education programs. *The Teacher Educator, 21,* 19-27.

Zetlin, A.G., & Hosseini, A. (1989). Six postschool case studies of mildly learning handicapped young adults. *Exceptional Children, 55,* 405-411.